Returning to Wholeness

Overcoming Life's Challenges
to Live a Blessed Life

Brenna J. Fields

RETURNING TO WHOLENESS
Copyright © 2020 Brenna J. Fields

All rights reserved. This book or any portion thereof may not be reproduced, distributed, or transmitted in any form or by any means, including photocopying, recording, or other electronic or mechanical methods, without the express written permission of the publisher except in the case of brief quotations embodied in critical reviews and certain other noncommercial uses permitted by copyright law. For permissions requests, write to the publisher, addressed "Attention: Permissions Coordinator," at the address below.

Printed in the United States of America
ISBN: 978-1-953497-02-4 (Paperback)
Library of Congress Control Number: 2020920354

Published by Cocoon to Wings Publishing
7810 Gall Blvd, #311
Zephyrhills, FL 33541
www.StephanieOutten.com
(813) 906-WING (9464)

Scriptures marked KJV are taken from the KING JAMES VERSION (KJV): KING JAMES VERSION, public domain.

Scriptures marked NLT are taken from the HOLY BIBLE NEW LIVING TRANSLATION (NLT): Scriptures taken from the HOLY BIBLE, NEW LIVING TRANSLATION, Copyright© 1996, 2000, 2002, 2003 by Holman Bible Publishers, Nashville Tennessee. All rights reserved.

Scriptures marked NIV are taken from the NEW INTERNATIONAL VERSION (NIV): Scripture taken from THE HOLY BIBLE, NEW INTERNATIONAL VERSION® Copyright© 1973, 1978, 1984, 2011 by Biblica, Inc.™ Used by permission of Zondervan

Scriptures marked ESV are taken from the THE HOLY BIBLE, ENGLISH STANDARD VERSION (ESV): Scriptures taken from THE HOLY BIBLE, ENGLISH STANDARD VERSION® Copyright© 2001 by Crossway, a publishing ministry of Good News Publishers. Used by permission.

Book design by ETP Creative

Returning to Wholeness

Contents

Dedication VII

Acknowledgements IX

Introduction 1

Chapter 1. What Does Wholeness Really Mean? 7

Chapter 2. What Happened? 13

Chapter 3. How Does Wholeness Manifest? 21

Chapter 4. How Can We Return to Wholeness? 29

Chapter 5. Trust God 39

Chapter 6. Dealing with Setbacks 51

Chapter 7. How Did I Overcome? 61

Chapter 8. Spiritual Warfare 69

Chapter 9. What is Failure - Really? 77

Chapter 10. Do I Love Me? 85

Chapter 11. Wholeness and Peace 91

Chapter 12. No More Shame 95

Chapter 13. I Deserve Better 103

Chapter 14. Life Lessons 109

Chapter 15. Live Full Out 123

Chapter 16. Conclusion 129

Chapter 17. Epilogue 135

References 141

Bibliography 143

This book is dedicated to

My parents: Alvin and Augustine (1944-2018) Fields, who instilled in me as a young girl that I could do anything I decided I wanted to do, and who set the example of living godly lives.

My grandparents and great-grandmother: Catherine Thomas Fields (Grandma), John Lemia Turner and Florence Brown Turner (Paw Paw and Maw Maw), and Venus Sample Prevost (Granny), who, each in their own way, supported me told me how proud of me they were. My prayer is that I continue to make them proud, even as they are among the great cloud of witnesses.

Acknowledgements

I first acknowledge and give thanks to God, in whom I live and move and have my being (Acts 17:28). I am nothing and can do absolutely nothing without Him.

I am grateful for my family and friends, who support me in whatever I set my mind to do. Thank you for your unending encouragement and love.

I must acknowledge the sister-friends who walked me through the challenging season of the last few years of my life. They checked on me, prayed for me, encouraged me, supported me, and were even ready to do battle for me. J.L., P.M.W. (RIP), P.K., H.S., T.R. and "25," thank you for everything!

I am especially grateful to Stephanie Outten and her team at Cocoon to Wings Publishing, LLC, who guided me through the publishing process as a newbie author, and who helped me feel at ease as I walked through unchartered territory. I am forever grateful for your guidance and expertise.

Thank you also to Shawn-Ta Wilson, who shared her publishing journey with me and encouraged me to pursue this dream of becoming a writer.

Lastly, I acknowledge every person who reads this book. I pray that God will bless you and speak to you through the words He's given me to write. Wholeness is possible!

Introduction

This book was birthed out of adversity, difficulty, and struggle. For women who have had the privilege of giving birth to a child, you understand first-hand the difficulty of the birthing process. You may have experienced morning sickness, swollen feet, weight gain, strange food cravings, elevated blood pressure or other manifestations of pregnancy. As the time drew closer for your baby's arrival, these symptoms may have increased in frequency and intensity. But then, the big day arrived, and you started to experience the physical manifestations of actually giving birth! Although I am not a mother, I have heard labor described by some women as one of the most painful experiences of their lives. I've also heard some mothers share that this pain can last for days! At the end of it all, an indescribable miracle occurs…the baby is born! Many mothers say that once their newborn is placed in their arms, the memories of the pain and difficulty fade. All of the negative and difficult experiences were worth it!

That is how I felt as I wrote this book! It has been a gestation and birthing process, and I praise God for the experience.

Each of us has our own ups and downs, and many times they come in seasons. We go through a period when all is going well…we have our health, good jobs, money in the bank, positive relationships…the list can go on. Just like the weather…one day it's beautiful, sunny, breezy, perfect. Our hearts are full of gratitude for such a beautiful day that God has allowed us to experience. Then suddenly, the weather report indicates that things are about to change. A hurricane is coming, a severe weather front is on the way and it's moving quickly! In the blink of an eye, things change. Just like the weather shifts, we may notice that our lives have shifted, and we've entered a different season, almost in the blink of an eye. We go from life being fulfilling, exciting and wonderful, to its being the opposite. We lose that good job we had, we experience a health challenge, we lose a loved one, our marriage fails. Sometimes these things happen one at a time, while at other times they hit us simultaneously.

And what is the aftermath of these life changes? It is similar to experiencing a weather disaster – tornado, hurricane, earthquake or something similar. After those storms pass, there is an aftermath. In the aftermath, many venture outside to see what damage has been done to their property and surrounding areas. Do we have roof damage?

Are all of our windows still intact? Is there water damage on our property? Do we have to live without power until the electric company can restore it? While the storm is over, the aftermath must be faced.

In life, we must first face the event itself (job loss, death, divorce). If there was a death, we have to face the immediate needs, such as the funeral. But what happens when the funeral is over, and everyone goes back to their normal lives? For the person grieving, there is an aftermath…dealing with our loved one's estate and processing our grief. And the aftermath is not just a day or two, but a season…

The challenging events that we face, along with their aftermath, can leave us in a state of brokenness.

The trials can be so severe that they seem to take a piece of us. We are never the same as a result of what has happened (or is happening) to us. We know that life as we know it will not return, so we grieve, mourn, and try to move on, but there seems to be an incompleteness, an emptiness, within us.

If your spouse decided he no longer wanted to be married to you, you may feel a sense of rejection, a belief that you weren't good enough to keep him and maintain your marriage And you may begin to feel and believe that you are less than.

Or, you may have had an idea in your mind about what your life would look like. Many women dream of having a lifetime of love with their soulmate, raising a family, and growing old together. While that is a reality for many (my parents were married almost 52 years before my mother went home to be with the Lord), it is an elusive dream for others. You wonder what you did wrong to not obtain the thing you dreamed and hoped for. Disappointment about the fact that life turned out differently than you envisioned can set in.

Or, you may have been working in a career for many years, and believe you are a strong contributor to your organization. Then one day, the company decides that your services are no longer needed. They help you pack the things at your desk and unceremoniously escort you out of the building. You are devastated and humiliated and wonder if all the years of hard work were worth it.

Whatever the situation is, something has happened to cause us to feel incomplete, less than, as if a part of us is missing. This is not a place we want to be, nor is it a place we want to stay. And this is not at all what God intends for us. So, what can we do to move from a place of brokenness to a place of wholeness? That is the purpose of this book.

Based on my experiences, I want to explore how we can return to wholeness. Why do I believe this a topic worth considering? First, I believe that we should each be in a place where we are content with who we are and what God is calling us to do. Each of us has a purpose and a destiny, and as believers in Christ, we have a hope and a future (Jeremiah 29:11). Yet sometimes our brokenness can get in the way of us being and living fully in the will of God.

Second, we know the saying, "Hurt people, hurt people." Those who are wounded and either don't recognize that they are, or know they are broken and refuse to get help, tend to hurt others, which then perpetuates brokenness. We see this in families that have suffered abuse. Those who have been abused tend to abuse others, and the cycle continues.

The good news is that the cycle can be stopped! I have learned that we do *not* have to remain in the state of brokenness We *can* break patterns in our lives so that they are not passed on to the next generation. The negative events that happened in our lives do *not* have to adversely affect us for the rest of our lives. In fact, we *can* allow our trials to empower us rather than to break and embitter us. With God's help, we *can* walk in wholeness, we *can* move toward the way God intended us to be and we can overcome life's challenges to live a blessed life.

Study Question

What do you want to get out of this book?

––––– ONE –––––

What Does Wholeness Really Mean?

One may define wholeness as "the state of being whole." But we've defined a word with a word, and that's against the rules, right? Think about an apple pie for a moment (my favorite kind of pie 😊). It's a combination of pie crust, sugar, cinnamon, and apples baked to produce a round-shaped, golden brown and bubbly creation. When it comes out of the oven, it is whole, and as we wait for it to cool down, it looks almost too pretty to eat! But the pie's purpose is not to be on display, but to be eaten and enjoyed! We cut that first piece, and while we enjoy its yummy taste, the pie is no longer whole. There is a piece (or pieces) missing. And eventually, it will be totally consumed. It is no longer in its original state.

When something is whole, it is complete and full, and contains everything it is supposed to contain. But life may happen to us to cause parts of us to be lost…confidence, contentment, peace to name a few. The difference, however, between us and the pie is that, once the pie is cut, it cannot be restored to its original state. Not the case for us! We may lose our confidence, purpose, or peace as a result of a storm, but the good news is that it can be restored! We can regain what we lost and be even better than we were before! That's wholeness!

There's a story in the Bible about a woman who suffered with an issue of blood for twelve years. Her body did not function the way it should, so in a physical sense, she was incomplete and broken. Not only did she have to deal with her physical ailment, she also had to consider the Jewish laws. According to this law, a woman on her menstrual cycle was considered unclean and had to ritualistically purify herself after her cycle was completed. Because of this uncleanliness, she was required to isolate herself form others. The woman's bleeding lasted twelve years, and because she had to alienate herself from others, she must have also felt a sense of loneliness. But she heard that Jesus was passing through her town, so she sought Him out that He might make her whole again: "For she said within herself, If I may but touch His garment, I shall be whole." (Matthew 9:21, KJV). She desired not only physical healing, but to be a part of society again. And she believed that Jesus could give her what she was missing and to make her whole again.

The gospel of Matthew gives us another example of a person seeking wholeness. Jesus and His disciples entered the synagogue one Sabbath and noticed a man with a withered hand. This man had something missing in his life…the proper functioning of his hand. We don't know if it was his left or right hand that didn't work the way it should have, nor do we know if he was right or left-handed. What we do know is his hand was withered, and we can surmise that he was unable to use it to its fullest capacity. In this story, what is important to note is that the religious leaders were also in the temple, watching and questioning what Jesus was about to do. The Pharisees were trying to trap Jesus into breaking one of the Sabbath laws which stated that no work was to be done on the Sabbath, and some scholars believe that the man with the withered hand was planted to assist with the trap.

The scripture does not tell us that the man asked for healing (I would imagine that he desired it, I know I would). We can surmise that he would long for his hand to be fully restored, so he could do all the things people with two working hands could do…farm, build, shake hands with someone, or any number of things. Jesus told the man to stretch out his hand, and "it was restored whole, like as the other." (Matthew 12:13, KJV)

Mark recounts a story about a blind man who sat on a highway near Jericho. Jesus and His disciples were in the area, and when a blind man named Bartimaeus heard this, he cried out for Jesus to have mercy on him. The blind man desired to receive his sight; he wanted to be made whole. As a sighted person, I cannot imagine what it's like to not have sight (once a year, when I get my pupils dilated by my ophthalmologist, I realize what it's like to not be able to see clearly, if only for a couple of hours). If we're blind, we may be dependent upon others to do things for us and are not able to see the beauty of God's creation. As a result of this limitation, the way God intended our bodies to function is incomplete, and our blindness may cause us to feel less than. But Bartimaeus cried out to Jesus to restore his sight, and the Savior did just that.

There are several examples in scripture of people who had a limitation (either real or perceived) and desired to be made whole and cured from their infirmity. This healing entails moving or changing from one state of being to another; in a physical sense, returning the body to how it was originally designed to function (eyes that can see, hands that can move, etc.).

The Faith and Healing Connection, a non-profit Christian health ministry, defines wholeness as "The state of being perfectly well in body, soul (mind, will and emotions) and spirit. This was God's original design for man before the fall and is now attainable once we join Jesus in heaven."[1] Unfortunately, we live in a fallen world, and as a result, are no longer in this ideal state. Because of the sacrifice of Jesus and the gift of salvation, we can be assured of returning to this ideal state in eternity. But what do we do while we're still in our mortal bodies? Are we still able to have some sense of emotional, mental, spiritual, and even physical wholeness - now? Yes, we are, by the power of God working in us to make us whole.

Based on the number of references a simple Google search locates on the topic of wholeness, this topic is something that is important to many people. We all want to be fully functioning human beings, without baggage and hang-ups that can hinder us from walking into our God-given destinies. Whether we realize it or not, wholeness is something that many of us desire.

Let me offer my definition of wholeness. I believe it is a state of being where a person is mentally and emotionally stable, is able to face challenges in a healthy way, and is able to rise above negative situations so that they can fulfill the calling that God has placed on their lives. Our lives may not be perfect (and never will be perfect), but a person who is whole can thrive despite obstacles that come their way.

Study Questions

What is your definition of wholeness?

_____

_____

_____

_____

_____

_____

_____

Look at your own life. Are you currently in a state of wholeness or brokenness?

_____

_____

_____

_____

_____

_____

_____

_____

_____

TWO

What Happened?

As we explore the idea of wholeness, we also have to look at brokenness. When we were born, we entered the world with no issues, no hang-ups, no concerns, no struggles. When you watch a newborn baby, they don't seem to have a care in the world. The only things they desire are love, food, and a diaper change. The newborn isn't concerned about the stock market, a 401K, the weather, or future goals. Life is simple when we enter the world.

But at some point, life happens (after all, we live in a fallen world). For some of us, it happened early in our lives, and for others, it happened in adulthood.

- As we are playing with our friends at school, we may experience rejection when we are the last one chosen for a team on the playground.

- We may strive for academic success, but encounter a difficult class and, as a result, may experience failure.

- As we get older, we will experience the loss of family members and friends. The grief we feel can be crippling and is life-altering.

- We may have our trust betrayed by a spouse or a friend.

- We made a bad financial investment, and as a result, experienced a significant loss of money.

The list of things that can happen goes on…

Each of these things can cause brokenness. Our innocence is lost, it seems as if a part of us is now missing, and we may feel like we're starting all over again. We may even blame ourselves because of the decisions we made. At the time, we thought we were doing the right thing, but time revealed those choices were not the best thing for us. And as we look back on our mistakes, we may realize that we missed some clues or signs as to why the choice was not a good one. So, we beat ourselves up for not seeing what looks like the obvious in hindsight.

While some of the things that happened to us were the results of our own actions, some of them were completely out of our control. We don't get to decide when a loved one dies, we can't determine when we will be laid off from a job, we can't predict when a health challenge will come our way.

All of these things, whether we control them or not, can cause our brokenness.

My story

As I reflect on my own life, I believe the events that have caused brokenness in my life are divorce, rejection, and death.

Having witnessed long-term marriages in my family (my parents were married almost 52 years, and my grandparents were married almost 68 years), I just knew that I, too, would have a long and satisfying marriage. I fell in love with a man in college, and although we would break up along the way, we reunited and eventually married. He was my college sweetheart and I loved him dearly. Unfortunately, after almost eight years of marriage, it ended. I was absolutely devastated. I did not want the divorce. Every marriage has issues, and I believed that if we prayed and worked on our marriage together, it could be saved. I recognized that I could have done some things differently, and I was convinced that we would be able to overcome our challenges and be able to share our testimony of success despite the odds. But that was not meant to be.

To say I was broken would be an understatement. What I felt was rejection, disappointment, and betrayal. I couldn't wrap my mind around the fact that someone who loved me could leave me. So, somewhere along the line, I internalized the false belief that I wasn't good enough for this person to love. I was less than, an incomplete woman. I masked those feelings by spending time with friends and busying myself with activities. I didn't fully process those feelings. I sought mental health counseling right after my divorce, but I don't recall doing very much with the information I learned in therapy. I jumped right back into life, thinking that I was completely healed mentally and emotionally. I now know that I was not healed.

Three years later, I met a man who was attracted to me in a short period of timey. I enjoyed the attention I was receiving, and the next thing I knew, we were in a relationship. I did not take the time to confirm that I was ready for a serious relationship, nor did I take the time to really get to know this person. I admit that I did not pray much about entering into a relationship with him. I was swept off my feet, and it felt good! I was no longer rejected. I finally felt good enough for someone to love! We dated about a year, got engaged and planned our wedding. Before the wedding, however, I began to see signs that something was amiss. I saw parts of his personality that I did not like – dishonesty, defensiveness, and keeping secrets (big secrets). We were very rarely able to have a civil conversation when we disagreed about something (my feelings were always dismissed, and the blame for the issue was typically shifted to me). This was a HUGE red flag, and sadly, I ignored it. We got married, which would turn out to be one of the biggest mistakes of my life. I was so desperate for my marriage to work that I glossed over these red flags and refused to address them. I even began to wonder if these things were of my own doing, and began to place some blame on myself, instead of assessing the true source of the problems.

Over the course of time, I came to fully understand that I was in an abusive relationship, and that my now ex-husband was a narcissistic abuser. I experienced mental, emotional, verbal, financial and even spiritual abuse. An understanding of spiritual abuse from the National Domestic Violence Hotline describes this type of abuse as one using religious texts or beliefs to minimize or rationalize abusive behaviors. Many things happened, but the final straw was when my spouse attempted to blame me for the many deaths that were happening around me (my mother, my godmother, a few cousins, an uncle, and a very close friend; all within a year's time). He said that "God is trying to tell you something" by allowing all of these people to die. While I knew this wasn't true, to hear those words, about seven months after my mother died and while my grief was still raw, was like a stab in the heart. At that moment, I knew I needed to get free.

All I wanted was to be a good wife and have a long marriage (just like my parents and grandparents), but that dream was crushed by lies, manipulations and betrayal.

Almost a year later, the divorce was final, but not without drama. Threats to take my home (the home I built before I met him), my business, to have me expelled from seminary, and to expose my secrets added salt to an already open wound. As the divorce process moved along (albeit very slowly), the mental and emotional abuse began to escalate. Because we were still living under the same roof, I was subject to things like verbal tirades in the middle of the night. I got to the point where I kept mace in my bedroom and in my car in case things became physical. I had to change the lock on the bedroom door and even began to hide my valuable, irreplaceable items (because he threatened to destroy some of them). I rode around with pictures of my late mother, valuable jewelry, and important paperwork in the trunk of my car for months. Sounds crazy; but I had NO idea what he would do while we lived under the same roof. Thankfully and praise God, none of the threats came to pass, my divorce was miraculously finalized, and I am now free. Sadly, even as I write this book, I periodically receive verbal intimidation from my ex-husband. When I filed a motion of contempt against him for not complying with the terms of the divorce, the verbal threats of exposure began again. Those threats mean nothing to me now and pray that God has mercy on his wounded and broken soul.

Each of you reading this book has your own story. No one's brokenness trumps another. We are all affected in some way by what has happened to us. No matter what the situation, I believe we can all see that we come out of our experiences different than the way we entered them. And we also must realize that, as we continue to live, challenges will keep coming, and they have the potential to compound our already existing brokenness.

So, what do we do with these experiences? How do we process them? What kind of people will we be as a result of them? We have a choice. We can remain broken, with the potential of inflicting pain on others because we are broken (hurt people hurt people); or we can choose to learn from the experiences, heal from them, and decide to return to wholeness. We can decide that the broken place is not where we want to stay, but that we want the brokenness to propel us to greater and better.

I can be bitter toward those who have hurt me, and even angry at God for allowing these things to happen to me. Or I can explore how these experiences can change me for the better. I have chosen the latter. I have chosen to allow these difficult experiences to catapult me to where God wants to me to be and to do what God wants me to do. Having been reminded about the brevity of life, I have decided to be better instead of bitter. This book is a result of that choice.

I pray you will decide to be better and not bitter as a result of your experiences, so you can return to wholeness.

Study Questions

What's your story? What happened to cause you to feel broken?

_____
_____
_____
_____
_____
_____
_____

As you recall your story, how does it make you feel? (sad, ashamed, embarrassed, etc.)

_____
_____
_____
_____
_____
_____
_____

THREE

How Does Wholeness Manifest?

Now that we have a better understanding of what wholeness is (and what it is not), how can we tell if we are on the path to wholeness? What things should we look for that indicate we're moving in that direction? As I reflect on my own life and progress on this wholeness and healing journey, here are some signs that showed me that I was moving forward. This is my list, yours may be a bit different. Whatever your list looks like, the signs we see should be moving us away from brokenness and toward wholeness.

Acceptance

There were several levels of acceptance. As I began to process the things, people and situations that caused my brokenness, along with my past mistakes, I began to accept them. I began to be at peace with the past. This acceptance didn't mean that I believed these things were good, but it meant coming to terms with the fact that they happened, and that there was nothing I could do to change them. They were in the past, and the past has passed.

Along with accepting the past, I also moved into a greater acceptance of myself. I acknowledged that I'd made mistakes in life (who among us has not), but those mistakes did not lessen who I am as a person or as one of God's children (read that sentence again). We are NOT our mistakes! Psalm 139:14 (NLT) is a scripture I quote often, and as I began my healing from trauma and brokenness, it has taken on a deeper meaning in my life. The psalmist says this: "Thank you for making me so wonderfully complex! Your workmanship is marvelous—how well I know it." The writer of this Psalm is thanking God for creating him in such a marvelous way. I wonder have we ever considered ourselves as marvelous. If not, it's about time we do! We are not saying this in an arrogant way, but we are humbly acknowledging that it was God who created us this way! God created me with a high forehead. I was teased mercilessly in elementary school because of it. He also created me to only grow to be a little over five feet tall. My family thought I would be tall because I grew fast as a younger child; but then I stopped growing at around 12. He created me with a relatively soft speaking and singing voice (which doesn't fit the Black Baptist preacher model of having a loud, booming, multi-octave, enthusiastic voice). Genesis 1:31 states that everything God created was good (including mankind)! So, in spite of my past mistakes, I accept me, with all of my flaws, imperfections, gifts, talents, and abilities. I accept the way God created me, even if other people don't like it. And I live full out, not hiding, lessening, or dimming down anything God has put into me.

In addition to accepting myself for who God created me to be, I also accept others for who they are. We should not be in the business of trying to change people (only God can do that, and we are NOT Him). People are who they are, and just like me, they've had their own issues, situations, and drama that have impacted them and how they see themselves. Accepting other people also means that once you see them for who they are, believe what you see and accept that as truth, and make the adjustments you need to make for YOU (please don't miss this point). If a person shows himself as selfish, believe him! If a person demonstrates that she is dishonest, believe her! Then do what's best for you; that may mean distancing yourself from her toxic nature and controlling how she is in your space, whether you only allow them in just a little bit, or not at all. Some people are so toxic that they can no longer be a part of your life if you really want to get your healing and wholeness back. This may be a difficult decision to make, but it is a necessary one. Loving people as

God commands does not necessarily mean having them in your life. We can accept people for who they are, pray and ask God to help them in their brokenness, and love them from a distance! AMEN?

Finally, to me, acceptance means that there is a great future ahead. Theologian and Professor of Biblical Studies, Tremper Longman III says this about Psalms 139: "He not only knows the psalmist's distant past, but also his future, a statement about God's foreknowledge." God really does have a plan for my life, and I not only accept this fact, I also await its manifestation by faith. Accepting that God has a "future and a hope" for me (Jeremiah 29:11) gives me optimism as I move forward to wholeness.

How else does wholeness manifest?

Peace - Shalom

Along with acceptance comes peace. I believe peace is more than the absence of conflict or difficulty, but that peace is a state of being. Have you ever encountered someone who is experiencing great difficulty in their lives, and yet seem to take it all in stride? We may say that the person is handling things with grace. Life is not easy for them (and they don't pretend that it is), but they seem to continue living in spite of. That person has peace. This true peace (shalom) comes from God and God alone. Look at the example of Abraham. God asked him to sacrifice his son (Genesis 22:2-3), the son that God gave him to fulfill the promise He made to Abraham back in Genesis 12. The website "Jews for Jesus" says this about Abraham and his situation:

> *"It seems beyond the comprehension of most people to follow such instructions at all, let alone to do so without anger, anxiety or despair. But Abraham obeyed God. He recognized that God had the right to require Isaac's life if He so chose. This trust and reliance in the One who created him made it possible for Abraham to have peace of mind, even when all his natural senses must have told him otherwise."*[1]

That's the kind of peace I'm talking about, peace in spite of what it looks like. A trust and reliance on God that does not change even if circumstances do. A peace that resides on the inside of a person and manifests itself on the outside. A peace that keeps us going, moving forward, and returning to wholeness.

Freedom

For those of us who live in the United States, we live in a country where we possess certain freedoms. We are free to worship as we choose, we are free to come and go as we please, we are free to live where we want. Of course, we can all think of instances where this may not always be the case, but for the most part, we live in a free country. Those are all outward freedoms, but what about inner freedom? If you have been a victim of domestic violence or abuse, you can relate to the fact that you were not always completely free. Someone may have tried to control your friends, your money, your thoughts about yourself, even your spirituality. For me, someone tried to control my thoughts about myself so that he could manipulate me. A person who experiences domestic violence or abuse feels trapped, feels stuck.

When we are whole, we are free to do, to think and to be. When I was married the second time, I felt I needed to dumb down to accommodate my ex-husband's fragile ego. I did not feel free to do, to think or to be myself. What do I mean by 'dumbing down?' I hid things about myself so that my former spouse would not feel threatened or intimidated by my words and actions. I held back on trying new things or engaging in new activities because I didn't want to give him reasons to complain that I was more focused on my goals than on him. I began lessening myself, but I didn't even realize I was doing it! Over time, I began to display less and less of my real self, especially around him. I am grateful that I have sorority sisters and a church family whom I could really be me with; but I still had to go home and live in an environment that was not open to accepting all of me.

This not only happens in homes, it can happen in churches, at work, and in families. For whatever reason, some people can't handle the complete you, and so they attempt to shut parts of you down to fit into their box or their idea of you, to make themselves more at ease.

Wholeness means being free to be ALL God has created you to be. It also means using EVERY GIFT God has given you to His glory. It means not being afraid of what people will think about the person you are and who you are becoming. It means living full out! Doing the most (as they say!) Doing YOU!

You may have some other words that describe how wholeness manifests. This is my list, and I pray these concepts resonate with you and help you move from brokenness to wholeness.

Study Question

What other ways do you believe wholeness can manifest in your life?

---- FOUR ----

How Can We Return to Wholeness?

Now that we understand what wholeness means, how it manifests, and the fact that we CAN return there, let's look at ways we can get there!

Who Am I, Really?

When we go through life's challenges, particularly when they are especially difficult, we are mainly focused on survival. How can we continue to function while we're in the middle of this situation? Our challenges can be all-consuming, and we may only have the strength to think about literally making it from day to day. And because we're focused on survival, we may sometimes get out of touch with the person we really are.

I know this was the case for me while struggling through a difficult marriage. While I continued to function at work, at church, with my family, and within the organizations I was a part of, it was as if I was on autopilot. So, when new opportunities were presented to me, I either didn't pursue them or I stepped forward and took them on secretly to keep peace in my home. I even ran for a regional position in my sorority, won the position, and served in it for two years - in secret. Lord knows I didn't want to hear more complaining and blaming than I was already receiving. Some of you may say "I'll never not be myself with people, no matter how they feel about me." But you'd be surprised at the things you do just to survive.

Now that my situation has changed (insert SHOUT!), I am emotionally and mentally free to truly be myself and embrace every part of me! Based on the lesson I've learned; I can never go back to the way I was! I am embracing every part of me by revisiting ideas and goals that I said I wanted to accomplish. One of them is this book! As I look back, part of the reason I didn't actively pursue writing was because my ex-husband had written a few books and I didn't want him to think I was trying to overshadow or outdo him or compete with him (trying to keep peace). But now that I am mentally and emotionally free from that situation, when I sit down to write, the words just flow (thank you God!)

As we discover (or re-discover) who we are, we can begin to set those goals, put them in writing, put a timeline around them and get them done. I am a follower of the ministry of Tera Carissa Hodges, who is an empowerment speaker, life coach and entrepreneur. Her ministry has been a blessing to me. (I encourage you to check her out.) A phrase she uses quite often is "it's time, people of God!" It is time to get started and finish those things we desire to do but were distracted because of life's challenges. We don't beat ourselves up because we got distracted; we recognize the issue for what it was, and as we return to wholeness, we pick up our ideas and goals where we left off and keep it moving!

As we rediscover who we really are, we may recall the things we used to love doing, but for some reason, no longer do them. Life got in the way, drama happened in our lives; whatever the case may be, somehow, we lost touch with our passions. As we return to wholeness, we can begin to reclaim those things that lay dormant inside of us and are a part of who we are. Do you love to sing? Start singing again! Do you love helping others? Start volunteering with your favorite charity again! When I sought therapy after my second divorce, one of the first assignments from my counselor was to write a bucket list. Two of my bucket list items were writing my book and taking dance lessons again. That list gave me something to strive and hope for when I began processing what happened to me. While I haven't started the dance lessons, the book is definitely here! Let's reclaim our passions and pursue them!

So, who am I? I am a daughter, family member, writer, teacher, speaker, singer, preacher, life coach, and community servant. And I am now walking in every one of those descriptors. WHO ARE YOU?

Counseling

In the previous section, I referenced the fact that I saw a therapist shortly after my divorce. And I'm not embarrassed or ashamed to share that with you. Right after my mother's transition, I participated in a grief support group to help me process her passing, and it has made the difference in how I have been able to heal (although I will always grieve her). There is NOTHING WRONG with seeing a mental health professional! As a minister, I wholeheartedly believe in the power of prayer, and I know God is able to heal us in every area of our lives (physical, emotional, mental, spiritual, etc.). I also believe that God has equipped mental health professionals to be used as vessels for our healing. They understand how our minds operate, and based on solid research, they can teach us coping strategies. If you are still judging people who seek counseling, then there may be something that you have yet to deal with in your own life (I'm just saying!). We MUST overcome the stigma surrounding mental health.

If you believe you need to talk to someone, do it! Check with your employer's Human Resources department to find out what mental health benefits are available to you.

Do a Google search for local therapists in your area and learn about what their specializations are. Read books and educate yourself. You can get free, but sometimes we need a little help.

Self-care

Self-care is a popular buzz word. Sometimes, when we think about self-care, we think about taking spa trips, getting our hair and nails done, or taking a fabulous vacation. All those things are great, but how often can you vacation to Paris or Greece or Africa (all places I want to visit, by the way)? What about those daily rituals, those small things we can do to take care of ourselves? Licensed Clinical Psychologist Dr. Maria Baratta says this about self-care:

- "Self-care means knowing who you are and your limits.
- Self-care means taking time to get to know *you* better.
- Self-care means taking time to love yourself."[1]

Visit her article "Self-Care 101" on the Psychology Today website for more on this topic. Self-care is something we should do DAILY. Many of us are nurturers and are always showing care and concern for others. But what about us? We've heard it before; you can't pour from an empty cup! We have to ensure we are taken care of, so we can then care for others. Self-care means being a little selfish, and that's OK.

Implied in the first self-care point listed is being comfortable with saying NO. We should not feel we have to prove ourselves to others by taking on responsibilities that we do not wish to. If we do not have an interest or the skill set to do something, self-care means saying, "thanks but no thanks," and leaving it at that (no explanation needed).

So, while we save up for that trip to Paris or Greece or Africa, we can still take care of ourselves. Self-care means that I love me and care for me!

Where's your tribe?

Sometimes, when we are in survival mode, we're so focused on making it to and through the next day, that we lose sight of our friends, our tribe. Now that we are returning to wholeness, it's time to truly reconnect with those who are our true friends, our "ride or die" sisters! These are the people who checked on you when you were going through, the people who prayed for you, the people who knew when you needed space, even those who were ready to do spiritual and physical battle on your behalf at a moment's notice. Now that your mind is becoming clearer, reconnect with them and find out what's going on in THEIR lives. They were concerned about you and now it's time for you to reciprocate. I'm not saying that you forgot about your friendships while you were struggling, it's just that your focus was on a different place. Thank your friends for being there for you when you needed them most. And don't delay! When I lost my mother, one of my close sorority sisters traveled to Louisiana for the funeral. The week I returned to Florida, she called to check on me. Less than two weeks later, she was gone (she died in her sleep). After I returned from the funeral, I said I was going to sit down and write a personal thank you to those who were my rock at that time, and unfortunately, I never got the chance to write that note to my friend and Soror Pat. While I believe she knew I was grateful, I wish I'd been able to put those words of thanks in writing.

Reconnect with your people! Suggest a girls' dinner at a local restaurant or host them at your home! Let them know that, just as they were there for you, you are there for them.

Discover your purpose

If you don't know what your life's purpose is, or had placed it on the back burner, now's the time to find it and walk in it! This is not a book about finding your purpose (there are many books that have already been published that can help you in this area). Once you believe you know what your purpose is, it's time to develop the skills necessary to be successful. If you believe your purpose is to inspire people by being a motivational speaker, why not look at ways to improve your speaking skills? Joining Toastmasters is one way to do that. If I know my purpose, but don't feel very confident about it, what can I do to change my mindset? Prayer and positive affirmations are what work for me to change the way I think about something.

Discover your purpose and walk in it! God has placed gifts and talents in you for a reason. The world needs what you have to offer!

These are just a few suggestions I offer to help you return to wholeness. What ideas do you have? Journal about them now. These things have helped me (and continue to help me) on my journey, and I pray they bless you as well.

Study Question

What things are you going to do in each of these areas to return to wholeness?

- Reconnecting with your tribe
- Self-care
- Goal setting
- Reconnecting with self

_____
_____
_____
_____
_____
_____
_____
_____
_____
_____
_____
_____
_____
_____

―― FIVE ――

Trust God

You have probably picked up this book because you've had an experience in your life that caused you to feel that something in your life is missing, that you are somehow incomplete. And as we deal with life's challenges and difficulties, we may ask these questions: "Where is God? Where was God when I lost my parent? Where was God when my spouse hit me? Where was God when cancer invaded my body? Where was God when I lost my finances? Why did God allow these horrible things to happen to me?"

As I struggled with the challenge of losing my mother very suddenly and coming face to face with the fact that I was in an abusive marriage, I would sometimes ask, "God, what in the world are you doing?" The day of my mother's funeral, a friend of mine told me that God was going to use what was happening for greater ministry. While I understood intellectually what she was saying, in my mind I couldn't imagine how that could be possible. Couldn't God have given me more ministry opportunities and influence in another, less painful way?

When adversity visits the lives of believers, we see where the rubber of our faith meets the road. We sing about, preach about, read about, and teach about faith and trust in God. But when life REALLY happens, this is the time to put our faith in action! But what if my faith is a little shaky at the moment? If each of us would be honest, we would admit that at some point in our lives, our faith was a little unstable. When I lost my mother, I didn't lose faith, but I certainly had questions. Let's not beat ourselves up over the fact that when tragedy strikes, we may question some things about our beliefs.

Look at the man in scripture whose brought his demon-possessed son to the disciples to be healed (Mark 9). The demon inside of the boy caused him to violently convulse! The father told Jesus that his son had been dealing with this situation, "since he was a little boy." And the father asked Jesus to help them, "if you can." We may bristle at the father's use of the word "if," but how many times have we used it in our own prayers and requests to Jesus? Can you imagine what this father is feeling? He is probably worn down physically, mentally, and emotionally from having to deal with his son's demonic possession, and I would imagine he was TIRED! Tired of not knowing when the next convulsion would come, tired of not knowing when this would all come to an end, tired of not knowing whether this demon possession would kill his son! Just TIRED! It's possible that the father demonstrated great faith in the beginning; he just KNEW that God would heal his son. But as time passed, the situation didn't change, and the demon tried over and over and over to kill his son. The situation seemed hopeless.

Despite the father's desperation, there still seemed to be some glimmer of faith. We know this because he sought Jesus and the disciples for help. If the father had felt all was lost, why bother seeking out someone who could assist them? So, even though the father said, "Jesus, help him if you can," there is still some measure of faith inside of the father. When Jesus questions the father saying "if," the father recognizes his weakened faith and says that he does believe and asks Jesus to "help my unbelief." (verse 24)

When our faith is unstable, we can ask God to do the same thing for us. Sometimes, our trials wear us down to the point where there seems to be no hope. I shared the difficulty I faced divorcing my abusive husband. The court process dragged on for about eight months, before we finally went into mediation in an effort to come to a mutual agreement on how to end things. As the mediation day approached, I prayed and believed that God would allow this part of the process to be amicable. I prepared myself for negotiation by considering what items I would be willing to give up in order to be cooperative in this process. The day of the session arrived, and I arrived early and sat in the parking lot so I could pray and bolster up my faith. As the process began, I learned very quickly that things were not going to turn out the way I had hoped. My ex-husband wanted to take my house (a home I'd bought before we married) and take half of the proceeds from my wedding planning business (among other things). He would not negotiate, and if I didn't concede to his wishes, he threatened to send a book he had supposedly been working on that would disparage my character to his book publisher. The mediation session lasted less than an hour, and we were at an impasse. And to say I was devastated at the results was an understatement.

The drive back home was a long one. And I will admit that my faith was shaken that day. I don't think I'd ever felt so much disappointment about something. There was no hope in sight that things would end any time soon.

Have you ever experienced a disappointment like this? We've done all we know to do, prayed, fasted, gave, and yet, there is no change in our situation and no hope in sight for future change. What do we do now?

Just like the father of the demon possessed boy, we profess the little bit of faith we do have and ask God to help somehow bolster and increase it. Many of us are familiar to mustard-seed faith. A mustard seed will eventually grow into a mustard plant of about six feet tall with sometimes expansive reach; but it starts off only approximately one to two millimeters in size. Jesus shared a parable about this kind of faith; He says that all we need is faith the size of a mustard seed.

"Because you have so little faith. I tell you the truth, if you have faith as small as a mustard seed, you can say to this mountain, 'move from here to there' and it will move; Nothing will be impossible for you." (Matthew 17:14–20 NIV)

Based on this, it seems that all we need is a tiny measure of faith. No matter how small it looks, as long as our faith is placed in the right source (God), all things are possible.

Back to our situations. Life may be hitting us hard, and we are overwhelmed, and physically, mentally, and emotionally drained. We seemingly can't take another thing! It's in these times, even with our little faith the size of a mustard seed, we can TRUST GOD! We may not have any answers or have no idea of which way to turn, but we can TRUST GOD! Let's look at a few biblical examples.

Abram – in Genesis 12 - was given a promise by God that he would be the father of many nations. However, his wife Sarai was barren. And they were both up in age (as my parents would say, they had a little age on them!) Yet, God made them a promise that Sarai would bear a child. She laughed at what she was told. They took matters in their own hands when it seemed God was taking too long and decided to allow Abram to have a baby with Sarai's handmaiden.

Despite their missteps, Abram and Sarai were blessed with a son, Isaac. God would change Abram's name to Abraham (meaning "father of a multitude)," which is in line with the promise God made to him.

Some years later, Abraham was told to go up onto a mountain and sacrifice his son. Wait a minute! I would imagine the loving father in Abraham was aghast, "Hold on God! We waited all this time to receive our blessed son, and now you want me to sacrifice (kill him)? That makes absolutely NO sense!" Yet, something in Abraham trusted God enough to pack up, travel up the mountain with Isaac and his servant, build the sacrificial altar, and tie his son on it and prepare to kill him! What was the reward of Abraham's faith? God had placed a ram in the bush, so instead of sacrificing his son, Abraham could sacrifice the ram. But on his way up the mountain, he had no idea what the end result of this trip would be!

As we experience our trials, we have no idea how things will turn out. That day, after the failed mediation attempt, I had no idea how my life would move from that point. We want things to turn out a certain way (in our favor), but we have no idea what will happen, when things are looking bad at the moment! As we walk day by day, every step is a step of faith, and a step toward the unknown. But the good news is this we may be walking into the unknown (because we don't know the outcome), but we are not walking alone. God walks beside us. And we trust that, as

He walks with us, He is guiding us to the outcome that is best for us. We still must have faith when the outcome is not necessarily what we want. We trust that God knows exactly what He's doing. He is an omniscient God. Even with our little mustard-seed faith, we are believing that all will be well. As Abraham walked up the mountain, Isaac asked the question "Father, where's the sacrifice?" He knew that they had everything they needed to make the sacrifice on the altar but the animal for the sacrifice. And Abraham answered, "The Lord will provide." Did the Lord not provide in the case of Abraham? Can the Lord provide in your case as well?

The Lord certainly provided for me! A hearing date was set to meet with the judge to determine our next steps in the case. Up until this point, my ex-husband had been uncooperative with everything the court required us to do (e.g., submitting the mandatory disclosure documentation). Both parties were notified of the hearing date, and once again, I prayed for God to lead me in the process. The hearing date arrived, and my ex-husband did not attend. The judge noted the history of uncooperativeness and his record of absences from hearings. From there, he took my testimony as to why the marriage was irretrievably broken, and my attorney presented evidence regarding the division of assets. No more than 15 minutes later, the judge pronounced the matter was closed, banged his gavel, and wished me the best. My attorney and I left the courtroom and gathered in a side conference room. I wasn't sure I understood what had just happened, so I asked my attorney to clarify; and her response was, "You have just received your divorce!"

Once the realization sank in, the tears began to flow! I couldn't help but think about the failed mediation session, when the threat of me losing almost everything was looming. And a month later, I was leaving the courtroom with everything intact, along with my freedom. I can still feel the emotions of relief and gratitude; that difficult process had finally come to an end. Although I was willing to negotiate and give up some things of value, God fixed it, so I didn't have to. Look at God!

One may ask, how do I trust God? In order to trust God, we have to know God. We have to know who He is as well as know something about His character. Who is God? This is a question that theologians have tried to answer for centuries, and we will not pretend to be capable of providing a complete answer here. But, based on my experiences over the course of my life, this is Who I've experienced Him to be:

- God has been a Provider of all of my needs (Jehovah Jireh)
- God has healed me mentally, emotionally, and even physically (Jehovah Rapha)

- God has given me peace in the midst of difficulty (Jehovah Shalom)
- God has always, and continues to be, with me. (Jehovah Shammah)

If you want to learn more about the names of God and how they teach us about God's identity, I recommend a great book by Dr. Tony Evans entitled, *Praying Through the Names of God*.

And what about God's nature? He is loving, forgiving, just, trustworthy, dependable, truthful just to name a portion. God has shown all of these aspects of His nature in my life!

So now, we may ask: "How do I know God?" He has given us His Word, the Bible, as insight into His nature and character. If we really want to know Him, we should make it a *priority* to learn about Him through His Word. We can also learn more about God from the testimonies of others who have experienced Him first-hand. Listen to what someone says who has experienced God's healing, provision, deliverance, guidance, wisdom, and deliverance. You can even look at my testimony. If God can do it for someone else, He certainly can do it for us!

We also learn to trust God from our own past experiences. Take a few minutes now to recall what God has already done for you. Try to remember in detail what was happening to you and how God brought you out!

As we are returning to wholeness, we are learning, little by little, lesson by lesson, to trust God more and more. Our faith may start off mustard seed sized, but as we progress, with Him by our side, our trust increases. Be mindful of your own journey and make note of how God allows your faith to grow. It will not be overnight, but you will see a change in you, who you are, and the faith you have in The One who can handle all things.

Study Questions

Look back on your own life; how has God delivered you from a difficult situation?

_____
_____
_____
_____
_____
_____
_____

Are you spending enough time in the Word to learn as much as you can about Him? Why or why not?

_____
_____
_____
_____
_____
_____
_____

―― SIX ――

Dealing with Setbacks

MANY MAY BE FAMILIAR with the expression: "When it rains, it pours." Or, as my mama used to say, "it's always something." We believe we are moving along well on our journey back to wholeness and we're starting to focus more on ourselves (not in a selfish way, but in a self-care way), we are getting the help that we need to get back on track emotionally and mentally, and we've set new goals for our new lives. Just when we think things are looking up, something happens that takes us by surprise, something that jars the sense of normal that we've been working to build and maintain. What do we do when a setback to our healing, and to our returning to wholeness, happens?

My setback was the passing of my maternal grandmother, whom we called Maw Maw (it's a popular New Orleans and Louisiana term, pronounced with a bit of a French accent 😊).

After my mother's passing in 2018, I took over care of my Maw Maw. She was already in a nursing home and was starting to display signs of dementia. She would continuously ask about my mother's whereabouts; she did not remember that she had passed and did not remember attending her funeral. In spite of the dementia, she was in relatively good health, taking only a few prescription medications. She had finally adjusted to life in the nursing home, and was very active in their Bible study, sing-alongs, and bingo games (which was her favorite). She was well-known and well-liked among the staff and residents and could regularly be seen engaged in conversation with some of the residents. She seemed to be maintaining relatively well, until the fall of 2019, when she contracted an infection that made it appear she was having a stroke. After spending a few days in the hospital, the doctors determined she did not have a stroke (thank God) and treated her with antibiotics. She got better, but then other issues began to come up. She somehow hit her foot, and the staff noticed that the bruise on her foot was not healing. She was sent to several doctors to determine what could be done, and they determined the reason for the lack of wound healing was poor circulation in her legs. Things became progressively worse, until it was determined that one of her toes needed to be amputated. A few days before Christmas, the surgery was successfully done.

The surgeon suspected that the amputation would not stop the infection in her foot from spreading, and he was right. Her surgical incision was not healing well (because of her poor circulation), and the doctors were now observing this infection spreading to other parts of her foot. At the same time, her memory began to deteriorate more, and she began sleeping more during the day. She would ask the staff to put her down for a nap daily after her lunch. She was no longer interested in all the nursing home activities – not even bingo.

There was no improvement in her condition as 2020 came in. By early February, the family realized that she may be coming to the end of her long life (95 years) and decided to place her under hospice care. Her hospice team was phenomenal, keeping the family informed of her condition on a very regular basis. A few weeks later, her condition began to deteriorate rapidly and on March 9, she breathed her last breath and was reunited with her husband, her parents, my mother, my aunt, and other family members in heaven.

Around this same time, COVID-19 began its spread into the United States, and just days after her passing, all nursing homes were shut down to visitors to try to stop the spread among the most vulnerable population. As we planned her funeral, guidelines for public gatherings were changing literally daily, and with that, so did her funeral plans. Finally, we were informed that we could only have a gathering of 50 or less of immediate family only. For someone who had been an integral part of a community for too many years to count, this was devastating news for us. The community could not say goodbye to her, a community she loved and loved her back, and our family was forced to grieve alone.

These events added to the weight of my grieving my mother's death. I believed, prior to Maw Maw's death I was handling it relatively well. Like most grieving people I had good days and bad days and came to understand that you never get over your loss. The uncertainty of COVID-19 added more complexity to this healing process. So, the questions I want to try to address are these: What do we do when we experience a setback? How do we ensure we continue to our journey back to wholeness, even in the face of a setback?

Setbacks may not only be life events; they may come in the form of mistakes (or what we may perceive as failures). Everyone makes mistakes, and we may not be the only people viewing missteps as failures, others may join us in that thought process. I have struggled with failed marriages and the perceived failure associated with them. After my second marriage ended, I began to question my own decision-making abilities. How could someone who has accomplished so much in her life be taken in by a narcissistic abuser? How could I have been so gullible and stupid? I've asked myself many times. And why did

I ignore the signs I saw ahead of time, instead of acting on them before marriage?

We can rebound from these setbacks and mistakes. But how?

First, we need to just *pause*. The Coronavirus forced me (along with the rest of the world) into a state of pause. All the things I'd be busy doing (teaching at church, sorority and community activities, events with my wedding planning company) have all been cancelled or postponed for the foreseeable future. Other than work and school, my life slowed down significantly. And the slowdown gave me a chance to pause and catch my breath.

Next, as we are in a state of pause, we need to *reflect*. Reflect on what? Reflect on the things that we've experienced (the good, the bad and the ugly). In his second letter to Timothy, the apostle Paul encouraged him to, "Reflect on what I am saying, for the Lord will give you insight into all this." (NIV) We should not only reflect on what has happened to us, but we should also ponder what lessons we can learn from these circumstances. One of the things I learned is to be intentional about taking time to reflect. I have neglected taking significant time to journal in order to process my thoughts and emotions. Journaling is something that my therapist recommended I do on a regular basis. I have also neglected engaging in quiet time with myself. And although I've gotten better, I've not been diligent to exercising regularly. Time to reflect opened my eyes to these conclusions.

Third, as Christians we need to *pray and meditate* on God's Word. Every Christian has heard this before, and yet somehow, it seems that we can't make it a real or consistent priority. Taking time to pray and hear from God through His Word is always needed, whether a crisis or challenge exists or not. If we are feeling that God is leading us to do something or change something, we need to hear from Him to confirm what we are feeling is truly from Him and not our own desires. In his epistle James, the half-brother of Jesus, reminds us that we can go to God for any guidance we need: "If you need wisdom, ask our generous God, and he will give it to you. He will not rebuke you for asking. But when you ask him, be sure that your faith is in God alone." (James 1:5-6, NLT)

In listening to the audiobook by Re-invention Strategist and best-selling author Marshawn Evans Daniels entitled "Believe Bigger: Discover the Path to Your Life Purpose," I've learned that setbacks are disruptions. Webster's Dictionary defines disruptions as "a break or interruption in the normal course or continuation of some activity, process, etc."[1] Something in our life has occurred that causes the normal flow of our life to be obstructed or stopped altogether. The death of a loved one can be a disruption, a layoff or a health challenge can be a disruption. This thing that has happened disturbs us, throws us off, interrupts us.

But I believe we should look at these setbacks differently. Evans says that disruptions can be a conduit for us to be re-invented! What a revelation! The events of our lives do not come as surprises to God. When we experience trial after trial, we may have been caught off guard, but God was not. We may feel a sense of disappointment that the progress we seemingly have made toward healing and wholeness has been lost in a setback. But we must remember this: there is a purpose for everything that happens in our lives, and we should lean into Him to understand more clearly what that may be. And as we draw closer to Him, He will speak to us, give us guidance, and provide us the peace that passes all understanding (Philippians 4:6) as we navigate what may seem to be setbacks to our return to wholeness. To God, these are not setbacks at all, but steps along the path He has pre-ordained for us. Our job as we maneuver through our trials is to trust that God will work ALL things for our good (according to Romans 8:28) and that He is with us along this life adventure.

Our setbacks and how we handle them can be a beacon of light and a source of encouragement for someone who is experiencing a similar situation. As we pause, reflect, pray, and meditate on His word, He will begin to reveal purpose to us, so we can move forward from our setbacks and into greater purpose for Him. I believe God has lessons for us to learn in all of our experiences. We can grow mentally, emotionally, and spiritually as a result of all of our difficulties. And yes, we can be re-invented!

I am looking forward to the re-invented me as I return to wholeness. Are you looking forward to the re-invented you?

Study Questions

What will you do to pause, reflect, and meditate on God's word as you process your setbacks?

_____
_____
_____
_____
_____
_____

Have you experienced setbacks in your life that would eventually reveal greater purpose in your life? If God has done it before, can He not do it again?

_____
_____
_____
_____
_____
_____
_____

Take some time to journal how you would envision who your re-invented you will be. What does that look like?

―――― SEVEN ――――

How Did I Overcome?

The years of my life between 2017 and 2020 can be described as a doozy! The hits kept coming and coming and coming! Shortly after returning to Florida after my grandmother's funeral one of my sorority sisters called me to express her condolences. During our conversation, she said to me "Girl, these last few years have been crazy for you! How are you holding on? How are you making it?" That is a very valid question! After our conversation, I began to reflect on the answer.

I prayed!
My prayer life grew to another level during that time! As I lived under the same roof with my now ex-husband during the process of our divorce, his behaviors became more and more unpredictable, erratic, and crazy. I had to pray for God's protection during that time. And I prayed that I would behave and react to what was happening

the way God would have me to behave and react. Did I always get it right? Nope! But I learned how to pray for my enemies, I learned how to do what Jesus would do, I learned to forgive. I learned these things because I prayed.

I praised!

It's not always easy to praise God when your heart is heavy and fearful. Church was not only an opportunity for me to worship God, it was a chance for me to get a break from a toxic living environment (although my ex-husband and I belonged to the same church, he very seldom attended). The opportunity to give God praise gave me strength! And even in the middle of chaos, mistreatment, and grief, I still had something to praise God for! I was healthy, I had a job, I had a roof over my head, my family was well, I had friends who were looking out for me, and so much more! And I could still praise God for who He is! Just because my circumstances were in flux didn't mean that He was! God is the same yesterday, today, and forever! Taking time to praise and worship Him kept me centered and focused on my Source.

In the book, "The Fierce Urgency of Now," author Eli Gonzalez shares his journey through a cancer diagnosis. He faced a diagnosis that most people did not survive (according to his doctors), along with a difficult treatment plan. This is what he says about praise: "When you unleash your praise ahead of knowing the outcome…a way out is revealed. Help comes from places you never though it would." As I praised through my difficult divorce, God gave me strategies to cope with the mental and emotional strain. He gave me supernatural physical endurance when I didn't get much sleep at night (because I feared I'd be awakened out of my sleep in the middle of the night by my ex-husband). And despite the lack of sleep, God still enabled me to get up at 4:00 in the morning to study for my Master of Divinity before my workday started at 7:00. God was faithful to me and provided exactly what I needed!

Praising in the middle of difficulty is hard. There were some Sundays I'd go to church and, although I knew I should praise God, my heart was too heavy to do it. The previous week may have been difficult, and it was all I could do to get to church, let alone try to praise. But somehow, I willed myself to lift my hands in worship to God. There was seemingly no end in sight for my toxic marriage, and very few people knew what was really going on in my life (in fact, no one at church had a clue during that time). I wanted to scream and cry out, "help me get out of this mess!" But somehow, I pushed myself to give God praise. I pushed myself to honor God for who He is and how He had kept me.

There is a praise and worship song that has become popular in recent years recorded by Bishop Neil C. Ellis and the Mt. Tabor Praise Team called, "I Command My

Soul." The lyrics talk about telling every part of a person's being to give praise to God.

I literally had to command every part of my being to give God praise because I was felt so low. But every time I did, I was reminded of the fact that God would see me through my situation. During difficult days, my praise helped build by confidence in God that He would protect me and keep me. The praise shored me up so I could keep going and face the unknown.

I trusted!

As I praised God, I also learned to trust Him more. I had NO IDEA how this divorce would turn out. Would the threats my now ex-husband made to take my home and business really come to pass? Would a judge be sympathetic toward him because I was the one who filed for divorce? What if I lost everything I'd worked for all these years? I had no answers to these questions; but I trusted that God would take care of me, no matter what happened! I will admit that there were some days when my faith was strong, and other days when my spirits were low. After my pity party when mediation didn't go well in our legal battle, I began to encourage myself. Just because things did not work out the way I wanted, did not mean that they would not work out at all! I had to remind myself that God was still sovereign and could still work this out for my good. I had to remind myself to trust God, no matter what!

I worked my ministry assignment!

As I shared earlier, many people had no idea I was in the middle of a toxic divorce. I was showing up for work, showing up for sorority obligations, and working my business (helping people get married even when my own marriage was falling apart). But more important than all of those things I was working my ministry assignment! Whenever I was asked to preach, I preached. Whenever I was asked to teach bible study, I taught. I taught my weekly Sunday School class as faithfully as I could. I kept doing what God called me to do, and every time, without fail, He empowered me to do it. God showed Himself faithful to me in this time, even when I didn't have the physical, mental, or even emotional capacity to do these things. After I finished teaching or preaching, I would have to pause in absolute wonder of God! I felt I had absolutely nothing to give physically, mentally, or emotionally, but I made myself available for Him to use. God reminded me during this time that I do absolutely NOTHING in my own strength. I had no strength of my own but somehow, I was empowered with supernatural strength that came from God. I kept working, and God was faithful!

Eventually, I would overcome! The things I experienced didn't kill me. In fact, they strengthened me, matured me, changed me, and helped me put things in their proper perspective. And as I reflect on those difficulties, I am grateful for the person I have become as a result of them.

If you are experiencing a challenging season in your life, I encourage you to remember these things. Never stop praying, never stop praising, never stop trusting and never stop serving. When there is no end in sight, God is there empowering you to make it day by day by day by day.

Study Question

What other things can you do (in addition to prayer, praise, trusting and serving) to overcome your difficult situation? Plan to start doing them today!

EIGHT

Spiritual Warfare

ONE SUNDAY, I WAS preparing to go to church. I'd gotten up early so I could pray to prepare my mind to teach my Sunday School class and also receive the Word from the day's preacher. As I was in my meditation time, all of a sudden, I began to feel sick to my stomach! This sick feeling distracted me from my quiet time before church. I started getting dressed, but the sickness did not pass, and I felt as if I wasn't going to make it to church that morning. Finally, I received a revelation of what was happening. Something was trying to keep me from getting to church to hear the message. Once I received that revelation, I began to pray and ask God to help me overcome this spiritual attack. I made it to church, I taught my class, but most importantly, I received the word that I needed to hear from the messenger that day.

I share this story because it is an example of spiritual warfare. One of Satan's objectives, according to author

Jerry Rankin in his book *Spiritual Warfare: The Battle for God's Glory,* is "to rob God of his glory in our lives." Rankin also says that "Satan will try to distract us, create doubts, and bring personal attacks to try to contradict the truth of God's Word." What does spiritual warfare have to do with the challenges we are facing? The Bible calls us to have the mind of Christ (First Corinthians 2:16), but our difficulties may be so challenging until we are unable to focus on having the mind of Christ. We are distracted from accomplishing the things that God has called us to do because we are consumed with our issues. This is spiritual warfare!

So, what's this warfare all about? Christians believe that there is a battle occurring between good and evil happening in the spirit realm. This battle has been taking place since Lucifer (Satan) was cast out of heaven by God. Satan wanted God's glory, and because he couldn't and didn't receive it, he now does not want God to receive the glory He deserves from His believers. While the battle begins in the invisible or spirit realm, it manifests itself in the natural realm. People do us wrong for no reason; they lie on us or gossip about us; we are tempted to engage in sinful behavior; we struggle in our faith; these are just a few examples of indicators that we are in a spiritual battle.

Just like any soldier, we use the weapons provided to us to fight so that we can be successful in winning the battle. The weapons of the Christian fight are not what one would think. We are not fighting with physical weapons (guns and knives) or any other earthly weapon. Second Corinthians 10:4 (NLT) tells us that "We use God's mighty weapons, not worldly weapons, to knock down the strongholds of human reasoning and to destroy false arguments." What are these weapons, and how can we use them to remain steadfast in the middle of spiritual warfare?

Ephesians 6:10-18 instructs us on how to fight a spiritual battle. The apostle Paul uses the analogy of the armor of a Roman soldier to teach us about our spiritual weapons. First, there is the belt of truth. What is truth? Christians believe that truth is found in The Word of God, and that God is truth. We believe He is the true and living God, and that the only way to be saved is through His Son Jesus Christ (John 14:6). This truth is foundational to what we believe. When we're preparing to fight, we stand on what is firm, solid, unshakable. We stand on truth.

The next thing we use in our spiritual warfare situation is the breastplate of righteousness. What is a breastplate? It is a piece of armor that covers a soldier's chest. It protects vital organs such as the heart and lungs from being injured. Our spiritual breastplate is one of righteousness, and this righteousness was not earned by us, but it was given to us because of Jesus Christ. Because Jesus came to the world and died for everyone's sins, we can exchange our sin for Jesus' righteousness. This divine exchange makes us righteous so that we are no longer condemned for our sins. We wear this in our spiritual battle to be reminded of who we are in Christ: that we are the righteousness of God (Second Corinthians 5:21). Knowing this fact can help us stand strong in the battle and protect our hearts of being exposed to the lies of the enemy.

In addition, we wear the shoes of the gospel of peace. Would you go anywhere (other than the beach) without shoes? Shoes protect our feet and allow us to step freely and without fear of injury while we turn our full attention to the battle at hand. It should be noted the sandals of the Roman soldier often contained nails or spikes so they could stay firmly planted in the ground. The Gospel of Peace is the message of Jesus Christ. As we fight our battle, we are fighting knowing we have the Gospel of Peace with us; and as we are engaged in overcoming our life challenges, people notice how we fight. This may cause them to wonder about our strength and tenacity, in spite of our situation. What a great opportunity to share the gospel with someone who is watching you go through your battle. And just like the Roman soldier's sandals, with the spikes or nails enabling him to remain stable, the shoes of the Gospel of Peace allow us to stand firm as we overcome our difficulties and serve as an example for others.

Next, we use the shield of faith. When we think of a shield, we think of a piece of metal that we can hold up to protect ourselves. The word of God says that our shield protects us from things that are being thrust at us. In the spiritual battle, our shield is our faith! Faith in what? Faith in God and His Word! If Satan tries to throw an accusation at us ("you will never be good enough" or "no one will love you again because of your mistakes"), we can throw up our shield of faith to stop it from affecting us. How do we do this? We counter Satan's attacks with The Word of God. Just like Jesus did during His time of testing in the wilderness (Matthew 4:1-11), we respond to Satan's attacks by saying, "It is written…" We can exercise our faith as we are in the middle of the battle.

Our next and only offensive weapon in this spiritual battle is the sword of the Sprit, which is the Word of God. While our other weapons defensively protect us during battle, our offensive weapon helps be proactive in the battle. The Word of God is the Bible, and it's our job as Christians to know as much as we can about it, so we can use it in the most effective way possible. We believe and stand on the Word of God as the truth that it is. The offensive weapon of the sword of the spirit can help our other weapons become even more powerful.

Now that we have our weapons for spiritual warfare, is there anything else we can use? Yes, there is! We can use prayer, which we are to engage in at all times! When we pray, we are in constant communication with our Commander (God), who gives us instructions as to what to do (or not do). Our job as a soldier is to be obedient.

In every challenge, I've had to engage in spiritual warfare and use all of God's armor to overcome. We must be intentional about using them. If we understand the fact that a spiritual battle is going on, and if we know how to use the weapons we have at our disposal we will, with God's help, be victorious. This is not hocus-pocus; this is an actual battle. While the spiritual contenders of our existence are invisible – as are those who war with us - we see, feel, and experience the natural manifestations of the invisible war. The good news is that we can win. We do not have to be defeated by Satan's attacks. Recognize what's really going on so you can fight well. Put on your armor. It's time to fight!

Study Questions

Are you in the middle of a spiritual battle right now? How are you able to recognize it?

What can you do to fight well?

―― NINE ――

What is Failure - Really?

I AM NOT A FAN of the word failure and its traditional definition. Dictionary.com says that the word failure means, "an act or instance of failing or proving unsuccessful; lack of success" or "nonperformance of something due, required, or expected." Webster's definition states the following: "omission of occurrence or performance," "a lack of success," "a falling short," or "one that has failed." I don't particularly care for the last description because it attempts to define a person instead of an act or event.

The definitions are so negative, don't you think? And I can understand why. It's not a pleasant experience when we don't achieve a goal we've set for ourselves. It's not good when we promise to do something for someone, but then fall short. None of us is perfect, so at some point in our lives we will experience this. And as a result of our failures, we can feel disappointment, rejection, sadness, displeasure, and frustration.

I believe that in order to return to wholeness, we need to view failure in a different way. I'd like to share a few quotes from several well-known thought leaders about the idea of failure. It is my hope that you begin to see this concept differently.

> John Maxwell: *"Everything in life brings risk. It's true that you risk failure if you try something bold because you might miss it. But you also risk failure if you stand still and don't try anything new.*
>
> *The less you venture out, the greater your risk of failure. Ironically the more you risk failure — and actually fail — the greater your chances of success.*
>
> *The more you do, the more you fail. The more you fail, the more you learn. The more you learn, the better you get."*
>
> **–Failing Forward: Turning Mistakes Into Stepping Stones for Success**

> *"Never consider the possibility of failure; as long as you persist, you will be successful. Remember, you only have to succeed the last time. It is not failure itself that holds you back; it is the fear of failure that paralyzes you. Failure is a prerequisite for great success."* Failure is a prerequisite for great success. If you want to succeed faster, double your rate of failure."
>
> **–Brian Tracy, Self-Development Author**

"Failure is a vital learning opportunity. Truly motivational quotes about success don't ignore failure – they focus on it. Rather than beating yourself up over a failure, learn from it and keep going. What you learned from the experience is likely to help you out in the future."
–Tony Robbins, Author and Motivational Coach

"Winning is great, sure, but if you are really going to do something in life, the secret is learning how to lose. Nobody goes undefeated all the time. If you can pick up after a crushing defeat, and go one to win again, you are going to be a champion someday."
**–Wilma Rudolph,
World Record-Holding Olympic Athlete**

I think you get the message! I believe it's how we view failure that will make the difference when we experience missing the mark.

When I became a certified pre-marital counselor, I was quite excited about the accomplishment. I had counseled couples before, but now I had more tools in my arsenal to help them prepare for marriage (not just a wedding). But sadly, not everyone shared my joy. A woman at church approached a friend of mine with what she believed to be gossip about me; she wondered how someone who was going through a divorce (at the time) could counsel couples about marriage. After all, the woman said, it seems that she can't keep her own house in order, let alone try to tell somebody else about theirs! My friend to whom the person shared this 'tea' immediately shut the gossip down (I'm grateful to have friends like this).

If I would have believed what the person said and decided not to pursue offering pre-marital counseling, I would be limiting myself and my gifts, and an important part of my ministry would be missing. Have I made some mistakes in the area of marriage? Child, yes! Have I learned from them? Yes! Because of my experiences in marriage and other parts of my life, I believe I am more than equipped to share with a couple seeking marriage what to do and what not to do in order to be successful! And I had the privilege of witnessing long-term marriages in my family. While neither of those marriages was perfect, each couple made it work. I am grateful for the real-life examples.

Brian Tracy believes that failure is a prerequisite to success; and I agree with him. Missing a goal, not achieving something we set out to do can be an eye-opening experience. However, it is not designed to get us to quit or give up, nor it is designed to affect how we view ourselves. Yes, we may experience disappointment and frustration when things don't go our way, but that has nothing to do with how we view ourselves. Failure is an external thing that does not dictate who we are internally. It may cause us to adjust our thinking so that we can achieve success the next time, but who we are as individuals remains the same. We are still fearfully and wonderfully made, even in failure. We are still loved by God, even in failure. We are still created in the image of God to do great things, even in failure. Missing the mark on a few things does not change who God created us to be.

Don't be afraid to try again! Take the lessons you learned from the previous attempt, make the necessary adjustments, and go again! Drown out and ignore the negative voices who don't believe you can succeed because you didn't make it work in the past. Evaluate your tribe and find some positive cheerleaders who support you when you try again. Step out and do what God has called you to do, even if it's the second, third or fourth (or the nth attempt).

So, what is failure, really? It's an opportunity to grow, it's a chance to try again, it's a chance to improve, it's another chance at success! This is how I see the word failure. What about you?

Study Questions

Recount a time in your life when you were not successful at something. How did it make you feel?

_____
_____
_____
_____
_____
_____
_____

How did you bounce back from failure?

_____
_____
_____
_____
_____
_____
_____

What did you learn in the process?

―― TEN ――

Do I Love Me?

WHAT A QUESTION! WE assume the answer to a question such as this would be yes, but is that necessarily the case? Sometimes, the experiences we've faced cause us to think of ourselves lowlier than we should (and I'm not talking about humility here). If we make enough mistakes (and because we're human, we make enough of them), we may believe that we are destined not to have a good life. If we are in an abusive relationship, whether it be with a parent, spouse, sibling, or friend (particularly a mentally, emotionally, or verbally abusive one), we may start to believe the negative things that are being said about us. And over time, these things may slowly chip away at our self-worth and self-esteem, until we don't believe we are good enough for anything.

The mistakes we make, and the negative things people say to us should not in any way affect who we are at our core! These are outside influences that do not change the person that God created us to be. So, what does God say about our identity, about who we are? As Christians, our identity is built on Jesus Christ...so who are we in Christ? I believe once we establish who we are and what our true identity is, we should have no problem loving ourselves. Do you agree?

Ephesians 2:10 (ESV) – "For we are his workmanship, created in Christ Jesus for good works, which God prepared beforehand, that we should walk in them." God created me to accomplish good works, and these works are already ordained (already set aside) for me to complete. The passage says that I am created for good works, not bad works, and not failed works. Therefore, I can be assured that, I am still called and assigned to go great things for God.

Romans 8:37 (ESV) – "No, in all these things we are more than conquerors through him who loved us." Because of Christ, I can conquer anything that comes my way. I am a winner!

Psalm 139:14 (ESV) – "I praise you, for I am fearfully and wonderfully made. Wonderful are your works; my soul knows it very well." This is probably one of my favorite passages in the Bible because it speaks to my very creation. To say that I am fearfully and wonderfully made tells me that I was created exactly the way God wanted me to be. He made no mistakes when He created me.

So, if we believe these passages from the Bible, what do they tell us about how we should feel about ourselves? We are to LOVE OURSELVES! And we can love ourselves because God loved us first. Because Father God loved us first, we can extend that love to others, according to First John 4:19. We have to possess love before we can share it with others, and that includes loving ourselves. I believe the passage also tells us that love is not based on performance but on being. The passages we've shared say, "we are" and "I am." They don't say "we do" or "we perform." Love is already inside of us, because of The One who created us.

Romans 5:8 says that "God showed his great love for us by sending Christ to die for us while we were still sinners (NLT)." John 3:16 (a very familiar passage) says that "For this is how God loved the world: He gave his one and only Son, so that everyone who believes in him will not perish but have eternal life (NLT)." Jesus was sent into the world by God the Father to die for our sins so that we could be reconciled back to Him and receive eternal life. Who among us would give up our only child to die for someone? Only God possess that great capacity to love someone, even someone who sins, makes mistakes, or experiences failure. In these passages from Romans and John, we see that God is the person taking the action; "He sent" and He gave." As His children, we can rest in that love, knowing that it is already there and does not have to be earned.

Therefore, since God loves us and has demonstrated that love, who are we to not love ourselves? We may have to forgive ourselves for past errors in judgment, but we should never condemn ourselves. No matter what people say or do to us, those things pale in comparison to what God has done for us. He gave His son, so I wouldn't have to be punished for my sins. What a loving and wonderful God He is!

And because He loves me unconditionally, I can love myself unconditionally. I hear you thinking: how can I love myself unconditionally?

- Get to know yourself – This means being honest with yourself, looking at all parts of you and accepting you for who you are.

- What do you like to do? What are some activities you'd like to try? What are you good at? Get busy doing all of it.

- Spending time alone – In your alone time, journal, talk to God, and enjoy your own company.

- Make a list of your accomplishments – remembering your successes will help bolster your confidence.

- Do things that make you feel good about yourself – polish your nails, try a new hairstyle or a new shade of lipstick, so that you like what you see when you look in the mirror

- Be intentional about doing fun and relaxing activities – take yourself to lunch, go to the beach, or take a hot bubble bath while listening to soothing music. These activities will help recharge you.

- Learn to laugh at yourself – we shouldn't take ourselves so seriously. When we are able to laugh at ourselves, we can accept ourselves completely.

I can accept me for who I am (good parts and not so good parts); and while I work to be a better person with the help of the Holy Spirit, I can love myself at the same time. I can be ok with myself; I can forgive myself; I can feel confident in myself and who I am…no matter what anyone else does or says. As we return to wholeness and healing, we unequivocally believe this statement: I LOVE ME!

Study Question

How do you feel about yourself, really?

_____
_____
_____
_____
_____
_____
_____
_____
_____
_____
_____
_____
_____

I encourage you to take some time to meditate on the scriptures above and ask God to reveal to you the depth of His love to you and for you, so you can then learn to love yourself.

―― ELEVEN ――

Wholeness and Peace

When we return to a state of wholeness, where we have accepted the things that have happened to us, when we begin to process them in light of the Word of God and look at them from God's perspective, when we begin to overcome serious challenges in our lives, we can experience peace. Peace is not the absence of conflict, but it is the strength to endure in the midst of conflict. We are able to live in a calm and tranquil state, whether we are experiencing tranquility or conflict. This kind of peace defies all logic; it makes no sense from a human perspective. Perceiving things from man's perspective, we should be all up in arms because of what we're going through. We should be worried, stressed out, not eating, not sleeping, with the number of gray hairs appearing in our hair growing by the week! But when we have the peace that passes understanding, our state is the exact opposite!

We can rest, we are not worried, we can continue to function (and function well), we are settled, we are content. And we don't look like what we're going through!

After my second divorce was final, I slowly began to share my experiences with some friends (my very close family and friends were already aware). The reactions from people would be remarkably similar. First, there would be a look of shock on their faces to learn what happened. Then after the initial shock, they would invariably exclaim, "but you continue to live your life? How did you do it?" One person said to me, "you wore your struggles very well, because I had no idea you were going through them." This is a testament to the power of God! I was able to live and prosper, not because of my own abilities and strengths; it's all because God *enabled me* to do it. And God gave me the peace to exist in a state of tranquility and calm in the middle of chaos. I could have lost my mind, I could have had a nervous breakdown, but I didn't.

How did I tap into the peace of God? First, I had to depend on His Word and believe it to be true. Philippians 4:7 (NIV) says: "And the peace of God, which transcends all understanding, will guard your hearts and your minds in Christ Jesus." I believed that God's peace would guard my heart and mind, so that I could continue to live a productive life. When things in my life were not peaceful, I would declare this scripture out loud, so it would resonate within me and I would believe it more and more.

Second, I tapped into the peace of God by listening to gospel music. I am a singer, so instead of singing the lyrics, I would listen to them to allow them to permeate my mind and heart. Lyrics to such hymns as "It is Well With My Soul" by Horatio Spafford or "Great Is Thy Faithfulness" by William Runyan would remind me of God's presence in my life and His love and concern for me.

Lastly, I tapped into the peace of God by visiting a favorite place. I love the water, so when things were especially stressful, I would pack my beach chair, my Bible and some headphones and head to the beach. Watching the waves and feeling the breeze brought a sense of calm to my mind. It has always been a place for me to meet God.

God will give you such peace that you become a living testimony for others. If she can continue, so can I. If she can make it, so can I! If she can overcome, so can I. That's when our life challenges are used for the glory of God.

If you are in the middle of strife right now, ask God to give you the peace that passes all understanding. Find practical ways to tap into God's peace. Then proclaim and walk in that peace as it manifests in your life.

Study Questions

Are you experiencing the peace that passes all understanding?

If not, what can you do to rest in God?

― TWELVE ―

No More Shame

WHY DID I STAY in a difficult marriage, you may wonder? I remained in a dysfunctional and abusive relationship because of one word: Shame. I was ashamed of the fact that this would not be my first time in divorce court. What would people think? Would they judge me? Would they consider me someone who was not worthy or capable to minister? And I was ashamed because it was difficult for me to believe that two preachers of the gospel (my second ex-husband was a minister as well) could not make a relationship work. Did we not have enough faith to believe that God could do anything? Even fix a dysfunctional marriage?

As I was in the process of the second divorce, I shared my situation with only a few people because I was ashamed that once again, I had failed at marriage. The people I chose to share my situation with never shamed me or made me feel bad, but even as I confided in them, I felt embarrassed and humiliated. As a Christian, I should have been able to overcome marital discord; I should have been able to make it work. Why couldn't I do it?

During this time, I began to do research on what I believed was going on in my marriage, and why I was experiencing certain behaviors from him. The degrading comments, the threats, the intimidation to get me to change my mind about the divorce (he threatened to call my seminary and tell them I wasn't 'fit' to receive their degree); the threats to take my home and business; the blame that would be pointed at me every time something would go wrong; it was always my fault. I wanted to try to understand what this kind of behavior meant, in the hopes that if I understood what was happening, I could employ different strategies to make things better. I don't recall how or where I ran across it, but the book *When Loving Him is Hurting You: Hope and Help for Women Dealing with Narcissism and Emotional Abuse* by Dr. David Hawkins absolutely freed me! All this time I'd been trying to put my finger on what could be causing the difficulties in my marriage. I even began to question myself. Maybe it WAS my fault. Maybe I WASN'T doing what God called for a good wife to do. There were times I even questioned my own sanity – when I would want to discuss something, he would flat out deny that he did or said the thing I wanted to talk about even with evidence staring both of the us in the face.

But when I began studying the book by Dr. Hawkins, all kinds of light bulbs began to come on! Missing puzzle pieces started coming together, and real explanations for what I was experiencing were revealed! After I finished the book, I felt I needed to find corroborating evidence from other researchers and writers about what I was going through (I wanted to make sure the author's work wasn't just an anomaly). Well y'all...it's not! I found countless articles, websites, blogs and books from counselors, psychologists, and even those who'd experienced this type of behavior first-hand. It's real y'all! Narcissism and emotional abuse are real!

Once I understood what was really happening, I then began to let go of the shame (this was a process...not something that happened overnight). I began to grasp that, while I am an imperfect human being and was, therefore, an imperfect wife (if you find any perfect spouses, please let me know ☺), I also received the revelation that no matter how imperfect I was, I did not deserve to be mentally, emotionally, spiritually or financially victimized. I began to process the shame I felt, and gradually came to understand that I did NOT have to hang my head in embarrassment and humiliation.

Releasing the shame of my experiences would also include no longer worrying about how my failed marriage would affect my ministry. Was I less of a vessel to be used by God because of the events of my life? Was it something that would disqualify me from being used at all? One day, during my mother's hospitalization, my Parrain or Godfather, stopped by the hospital to take me to lunch. When we returned to the hospital and we began to chat in the waiting area, I confided in him that I had started thinking about divorce and gave him some insight into what was happening in my marriage. As a retired pastor and leader in the United Methodist Church, I greatly value his insight on all things ministerial. When I asked him how he thought my filing for divorce would affect my ministry, he said very simply and emphatically, "Don't worry about that!" He reminded me that God was sovereign, and that He would handle those things at the appropriate time. I can honestly say that my Parrain was right! A part of releasing the shame of my experiences was trusting in the fact that what God has for me, it's for me. If God intends for me to be used as a vessel for His glory for His kingdom, He and He alone will make that happen. As time has progressed from that day, God has been faithful in using this willing vessel for His glory, and for that, He gets all the praise!

Another aspect of shame I had to release was the concern about what others thought about me. In self-reflection I realized that for a good portion of my life, I was worried about what people thought of me. I've always been the type of person who likes getting along with everybody. But could it be that in my quest to get along with everybody, my focus started shifting to fitting into boxes of other people's making, so that I would be liked? It has taken me most of my adult life to realize that the last thing on my mind should be what other people think about me! (Revelation and Freedom!) God already loves me, so I don't have to try to earn His feelings for me. The only other person whose love and acceptance I need and should seek out is ME!

And because God loves me and I love myself, I do not have to experience shame. And why not? Because of my identity in Christ. God did not create me to live in shame and guilt, as if I were unworthy. I *am* worthy because of the fact that God created me and sent His Son to die for my sins. I *am* worthy because He fearfully and wonderfully made me (Psalms 139). I *am* worthy because He has given me gifts and abilities that need to be shared with the world.

Shame causes one to hide. But, once I processed my feelings, I realized that "ashamed," "humiliated," or "embarrassed" are no longer words I use to describe myself. I am no longer ashamed of my past or my mistakes. I am sharing my story with other people because the shame is gone, and I feel compelled to share with others about how God delivered me from abuse, is healing me from grief, and is returning me to wholeness. I am free to be the person God has called me to be so I can help someone else who is experiencing a similar plight.

I recognize that there may be some people who will judge me and won't be able to look beyond my experiences. They may even disqualify me because of them. Oh well! God has already ordained my purpose, and I am going to walk in it, no matter how others may judge me. God bless them!

I now understand that the challenges I've experienced in my life are connected to my assignment, connected to the purpose God has ordained for me! God allowed these experiences so that I could be better, wiser, and stronger for my God-given work for His Kingdom. And because of that, I no longer need to be ashamed!

No More Shame! I'm FREE! Free to be who God created me to be, free to accept me for who I am. No More Shame! Thanks be to God!

Study Question

What are you ashamed of about yourself? Be honest as you answer this question. Pray and ask God to free you from this shame.

_____
_____
_____
_____
_____
_____
_____
_____
_____
_____
_____
_____
_____
_____
_____
_____

THIRTEEN

I Deserve Better

I ALMOST DIDN'T WRITE THIS chapter. The idea came to me that I should include it, but whenever I would sit down to write it, I would decide not to, and move on to work on something else. As I reflect on the reasons why I was hesitant about this chapter, this thought came to mind: Maybe I was apprehensive about writing it because it meant I would have to admit something to myself that I didn't want to articulate. I would have to acknowledge that, in some areas of my life, I settled for less than what I deserved. I would have to own that part of me.

Something within told me it was okay to accept less. Although there have been times when I've felt less than confident about me, I would say that my level of self-esteem was probably average. I've always been assured and comfortable about myself in academics and in the gifts and talents that God has given me. But it is the areas of my appearance and being liked by others that I struggle. In addition, I was worried about fitting in. And sometimes, in my effort to fit in, I may have settled for something that I shouldn't have.

The fact that I deserve better is probably one of the greatest lessons I've learned from my season of trials and tests. I now understand that I am worth more than I believed before. As I wrote this chapter, these statements began to flow from my mind to the keyboard, like water falling from a waterfall:

- I do not have to settle for just anything or anyone.
- God has special blessings set aside just for me.
- I am more than enough.
- I am because God is.
- I trust God for the best things in my life.
- I deserve the best.
- I will not settle for less than just to have something. I'll wait on the real blessing and not settle for a substitute.
- I will receive everything that God intends for me to have.
- I trust God to bring all of His promises in my life to pass.
- I already have within me everything I need to do what God has called me to do.
- I deserve better.

This chapter is especially for those who, despite the fact that you've been successful, and that life has generally been good, somewhere over the course of your life, you've settled for less than you deserve. It could have been a mate, a friendship, a job or whatever. I want to help you dispel the wrong thinking that anything is better than nothing. I want to help you change your mindset.

I encourage you to use these affirmations (and come up with your own) to shift your thinking and beliefs about what you deserve. It doesn't matter what your life looks like right now. No matter what life throws at you, your inner self should still believe that "I deserve better." No matter what the world says, I deserve the best of what God has for me. No matter what has happened to me, I deserve to live a fulfilling life. And I deserve this because of the love of God!

Protecting our minds is something we have to practice on a regular basis. The devil will try to introduce thoughts that have no business being there. We have to work actively and intentionally to feed our minds and hearts with the positive, so that when the negative is tossed at us, we can rebuke it. And one of the thoughts we must continuously believe is "I deserve better."

As we journey back to wholeness and gain a sense of peace, we come to realize that we should no longer settle for things we've accepted in the past. Journeying back to wholeness is growth and maturity, and with that maturity comes the application of hard-earned lessons. One of which is "I deserve better."

No more settling…no more compromising…no more conceding. I deserve better!

Study Question

In what areas of your life have you settled? Make up in your mind TODAY that you will no longer compromise, because you realize you deserve the best!

─── FOURTEEN ───

Life Lessons

Out of every experience, we should be able to discern some lessons. God does not allow us to go through challenging times for us to remain the same; in some way, we should be different individuals after we've gone through and come out on the other side. As you return to wholeness, take the time to reflect on what has happened and what you have learned along the journey. In my experiences with disappointment, failure, death, and divorce, these are my lessons:

Listen to the voice of the Holy Spirit when He speaks.

Believers in Christ possess the Holy Spirit who lives on the inside of us. His job is to be our helper (John 14:26), provide us with wisdom (1 Corinthians 2:10-11), give us spiritual gifts (1 Corinthians 12:4), and provide us with hope (Romans 15:13). Note: this is not an exhaustive list, but it gives you an idea of the role of the Holy Spirit in the life of the believer.

You may encounter a situation or a person where something just doesn't feel right. For example, someone may say something to you that you just can't fully believe. A question mark pops up in your mind, and you begin to say, "Hmmm." The lesson I've learned is if your spirit is unsettled about a person or a thing, don't ignore this feeling. If a person shows you who they are by their actions, believe the actions! If a person has lied, be watchful so you can determine if they are, by nature, a liar. If a person loses their temper once or twice, be observant that this does not become a pattern. If it does, you are seeing a person's true nature. This is the Holy Spirit speaking to you, trying to impart wisdom to you. Reviewing my own life, I saw glaring caution signs that indicated I should've proceeded guardedly. Unfortunately, I did not; and that action caused me to go down a road that I never imagined. Trust that inner voice, the Holy Spirit, who is speaking to you, leading you, and even warning you of impending danger.

Take your time; don't rush

Related to the first point is this one: Don't rush into making major decisions; take your time. When I met my ex-husband, I fell for him quickly. He was kind, intelligent, funny, and caring. He was a believer, which was an important quality for me. Although I didn't realize it at the time, I was glad someone was interested in me. Past relationships had adversely affected my self-esteem, and was still impacted by rejection, which will do a number on you. Things moved very quickly, and I attributed that to the fact that we were not 20-year-olds and were mature enough to decide to be in a relationship and not waste time dating. I was showered with attention, quality time, gifts, dates (just to name a few), and I just knew this was it! This was the relationship for me!

Hindsight has taught me a couple of things. First, I now know that I was being love bombed. In the article "Love Bombing: A Narcissist's Secret Weapon" in Psychology Today, author Suzanne Degges-White defines love bombing as "the practice of overwhelming someone with signs of adoration and attraction."[1]

The author goes on to say that, "Not everyone who whispers sweet nothings in your ear is a narcissist or predator, of course, but if you're feeling that something just isn't right about the person or your relationship, these constant reminders of 'how good you are together' — when you suspect that you really aren't — can be an effort to keep you tethered. It's often the first line used by a potential abuser."

This is what was happening to me! If I'd slowed down the pace of our relationship so I could process the things that the Holy Spirit was showing me, the situation may have turned out differently.

In addition to taking our time in making important decisions, we should also take our time as we recover from difficult situations. Grieving traumatic experiences and their aftermath can take time, and we should afford ourselves the opportunity to work through this grief. Grief comes as the result of a loss; it could be the loss of a loved one, the loss of opportunities, the loss of previous versions of ourselves, or the loss of dreams. There is no timeline for a person to finish grieving and the grief process looks different for each of us, so we should give ourselves grace as we walk through this season. I've grieved the loss of loved ones, the loss of the opportunity to have a long marriage like my parents and grandparents, and the loss of the idea of what I believed my life would look like. I've learned the importance of taking time to grieve these losses so I can move forward into what God has for me. And I've learned to be patient and gentle with myself as I process my grief.

If you are experiencing the loss of a loved one, I highly recommend Grief Share. It is a Bible-based support group that helps people navigate through the experience of grief. The support I received from Grief Share as a participant (and now as a facilitator) has been a blessing to me, and I pray it will help you as well.

So, take your time. There's no need to rush through anything. What God has for you is not going to disappear if it's truly meant for you to have.

Speak up for yourself!

When God shows us something to act on, we should not be afraid to speak up and address those issues. As my marriage progressed, I spoke up for myself to confront issues less and less, because I was trying to keep peace in my home. When there was no peace at home, there was constant blaming (gaslighting) and constant lying. Some days it was just easier to not confront. But as I look back, trying to keep the peace in this way really did not create peace. I was just walking around on eggshells, waiting for the next blow-up, waiting for the other shoe to drop. This is no way to live.

If you are in an abusive relationship, care should be taken so that you are not endangering yourself with your communication. I do believe it is important to have free communication in a relationship, and each party should feel comfortable expressing themselves. As I look back over both my marriages, there were instances where I should have expressed myself sooner, when issues arose. Confront issues as they occur, don't allow them to fester, and if you feel you are in a harmful situation, please take care in doing so.

Seek wise counsel / mental health counseling

We currently live in a time where awareness of the importance of mental health is increasing. In the past, people were ashamed to admit that they were struggling mentally and felt as if addressing mental health challenges could be perceived as a weakness. As you return to wholeness, you may realize that you can't do it alone. Yes, prayer is important, and as a minister, I am a strong advocate for prayer. However, Christians *must* stop believing that prayer is our only avenue for healing. God has given mental health professionals the knowledge to understand how the human mind works so that they can help us in this area. Why not pray *and* seek counsel?

Seeking wise counsel can be as simple as reaching out to a friend who has had a similar experience, or it could be attending counseling sessions with a professional counselor or therapist. Whatever it looks like for you, seek this wise counsel. Pray and ask God to lead you to the right person: someone who will keep your confidence and who will not judge you but love you through your difficulty. I am extremely grateful for the wise counselors in my life, who at one point included a licensed mental health professional. My second therapist was a Christian counselor (if you are Christian, I recommend you seek a Christian counselor) who helped me understand my situation from a biblical as well a clinical standpoint. I am also thankful for my girlfriends, who were ready and willing to support me in a way they could. They were my sounding board and my guidance when my mind was cloudy. For example, one of them suggested I get mace when I began to feel unsure about my physical safety at home. I had never considered getting mace before (or needing it for that matter). But her advice made sense; I needed to be able to protect myself, just in case.

A lesson I learned about seeking wise counsel is the importance of heeding wise counsel's advice. My first husband and I sought counseling together in an effort to save our marriage; when the relationship ended, I continued seeing this therapist, so I could focus on my healing. Unfortunately, I did not follow her advice of taking time to reflect on the past so I could learn from it. Several months after my first divorce, I began seeing another person, thinking that I had moved passed my hurt, when I really had not. I may have moved forward with a new relationship differently if I'd listened to my therapist's advice.

Take your healing seriously! Don't downplay its importance because this is about you and your future!

Maintain your friendships

Maintain your friendships and relationships, even while you're going through difficulties. Don't allow another person to alienate you from those who support you the most. If I had not maintained my friendships through my challenges, who would have been there to provide wise counsel and support when I needed it? As I look back, I can see instances where my ex-husband tried to alienate me from those closest to me. For example, he insisted that my cousin was jealous of me. I never saw that behavior in her, but he tried to convince me that she envied me and the life I lived. The fact of the matter is she and I both lived blessed lives, so what would be the need for her jealousy? I am grateful that I didn't fall for that lie (listening to the Holy Spirit told me that this was not true). Those who seek to manipulate us want to get us alone so they can do what they will; do your best to not allow this to happen. Make time to spend with your friends and those who care about you (or at minimum, stay in touch with your friends) and, continue to do the things you enjoy doing.

It's okay to be alone

This is a lesson I'm learning, even as I write this book. I am returning to wholeness in my life, and a part of this return is spending time alone. Yes, it's important that we maintain our friendships and relationships. And while I hope to enjoy a romantic relationship again one day, I am good with spending time alone. My alone time has helped me process the things that have happened, so I can heal from them. And I am in fact healing. People are expressing that they see it, "You look happy" and "You look like you are loving yourself." And my response is always a resounding YES! I am reflecting, I am processing, I am learning, I am letting things go, I am finding myself again, I am embracing who I am again. And I'm able to do that because I'm spending time with me! Don't neglect this! It's okay to spend time alone.

Trust God in adversity

In the middle of adversity, we learn lessons we would not have otherwise received. One of the most important lessons for me was adversity taught me how to pray deeper and to trust God more. When your back is against the wall, and there is literally nothing you can do to help yourself, you recognize that God is your source! So, you cry out to Him for deliverance. Then you trust that He *will* deliver, not in your time, but in His.

In her Our Daily Bread devotional message, writer Linda Washington wrote: "Hardship is often the process by which God purifies the gold of our faith. In our pain we might beg God to quickly end the process, but He knows what's best for us, even when life hurts."[6] When God purifies us through adversity, we must trust that He has our best interest at heart, and that He will not allow us to be destroyed in this process.

In all of my challenges, I had to trust God, even when I saw no end in sight. And I had to believe that He would protect me, care for me, supply all my needs, and most importantly, never leave me. And He did exactly that!

Learn the difference between happiness and joy

The various experiences in my life have taught me the difference between happiness and joy, and as I continue to mature spiritually, the distinction between the two concepts is becoming even more clear. I believe that happiness is an emotion that is predicated upon good things happening in our lives. When we are healthy, we can be happy. When we have a good-paying job, we can be happy. When we are debt-free and secure financially, we can be happy. But what if those things change or disappear from our lives? When we lose that good-paying job, our feelings change. We may begin to worry about how we're going to pay our bills. Our emotional state has changed from happiness to worry because our life circumstance changed.

But what about joy? Joy is one of the Fruit of the Spirit that the Apostle Paul teaches: "But the Holy Spirit produces this kind of fruit in our lives: love, joy, peace, patience, kindness, goodness, faithfulness, gentleness, and self-control. There is no law against these things!" (Galatians 5:22-23, NLT) As Christians, this Fruit is something that we have access to, because the Holy Spirit resides inside of us. I define joy as a contented state of being, where we experience peace of mind, no matter what the circumstance. So, if we lost our good health or our good job, we could still have joy. We have joy because we trust that, no matter what happens to us, God is in control and He has promised in Psalm 55:22 (NLT) that we can "Give [our] burdens to the Lord, and he will take care of [us]."

If I had to choose between happiness and joy, I would choose joy. My joy is consistent, and it remains no matter what. The source of my joy is God, who does not change. If the source of my joy doesn't change, then neither should my joy.

I never would have asked for the life experiences I've had to happen to me. But God allowed all of them, and He has used them for His glory and for my benefit. Not only have I learned lessons from these experiences, but I have changed. I am a different person. In what ways am I different?

First, my *prayer life* has changed. I have become a greater intercessor. When someone says that they have lost a mother or a grandmother or someone close to them, or if someone says they were (or are) in an abusive relationship, I can immediately relate. While our situations may not be exactly alike, there are some real similarities. Just like so many prayed for me through these difficulties, I am compelled to "pay it forward" and pray for others. These prayers are more than "Lord, bless so and so." They are specific! Because I now understand the nuances of these situations, I can pray in ways I wasn't able to before.

Related to the first way I've changed is the fact that I am now *more compassionate*. I considered myself a compassionate and caring person before, but now that feeling is almost on steroids! My heart hurts along with people who are hurting, and I can share my own experiences in the hopes that they will help someone else.

Lastly, I'm different because my *faith* is different. My faith is stronger. In the dark days of my divorce, when I didn't know when the end would come, when I didn't know what craziness my ex was going to say or do to me, or what lie he was going to tell, I had to believe by faith that this situation would eventually come to an end. I trusted God to be my Advocate and my Defender when things seemed hopeless, when I thought I might lose everything. I had to trust that God saw what was happening and would protect me from threats and unfair behavior. I trusted God, and He came through!

All the things I share that happened to me were hard and, I am still processing some of them. And I wouldn't wish any of them on my worst enemy. But I can honestly say, I am grateful in each of them. I now understand what 1 Thessalonians 5:18 (NLT) really means: "Be thankful in all circumstances, for this is God's will for you who belong to Christ Jesus." The passage doesn't say to be thankful FOR all things, but it says to be thankful IN all things. No, I am not thankful that my mama made her transition, but I am thankful for what I've learned and who I've become in the process. As I write this section, the world is in the middle of a global pandemic (coronavirus), and we are all ordered to stay at home. As a kidney dialysis patient, my mother was in a delicate health situation. While I miss her greatly, I am thankful that she is not in this earth to be susceptive to COVID-19. God has shielded her from the virus, and for that I am thankful.

As you are experiencing your trials, take some time to find out what God is trying to teach you in this. Ask Him to show you what the lessons are. Then apply those lessons so you can be even more fit for kingdom service.

Study Questions

What is God trying to teach you in this season?

How are you different as a result of your experiences?

―― FIFTEEN ――

Live Full Out

MANY YEARS AGO, IN my teenage years, I danced with an amateur ballet company in New Orleans called Ballet South of New Orleans. I fell in love with ballet at age seven, when the woman who would become my dance teacher came to my elementary school and performed. I ran home after school telling my mother that I had decided what I wanted for my eighth birthday (that was coming up in the next month). I told her I wanted ballet lessons for my birthday gift. I remember her saying something like, "oh really!" 😊 I excitedly told her how great it was to see the ballerinas dance across the stage and that I wanted to be able to dance just like them! I would later find out that my parents had already decided on my birthday gift that year (a puppy), but I also got the ballet lessons!

Ballet still has an influence on my life even over 40 years later. It taught me grace, taught me how to carry myself, and exposed me to classical music that I would one day learn to play on the piano and enjoy to this day (even though I very seldom play). One of the lessons from ballet I am re-discovering is the concept of dancing full out. Dancing full out means to not mark the steps or to walk through the choreography, but to dance with all your energy and heart. There were times that called for us to "mark it," and yet other times where we were expected to dance in rehearsal as if we were performing on stage in front of a packed audience.

How does this concept apply to life? Life is not a dress rehearsal or practice. We only get one opportunity to live in this world. And while we are here, we should LIVE FULL OUT!

As I look back over my life, I realize there were times I was not living full out. Thank you, God, for hindsight and revelation! Guess what, y'all? I ain't doing that no mo' (bad grammar intended)! The reason you are reading this book is because I decided to live full out! The reason I am trying new things is because I have decided to live full out. Life is too short, and God has given me too many gifts to allow them to lie dormant to make others more comfortable with me!

As I am beginning to live full out, I am reflecting on what my mother would regularly say about me. She always told me I was a special child because I was born with a veil (or caul) on my face. There are several cultures that believe that babies born that way are special and gifted. As I researched this, I found an interesting article by Giselle Castro about this phenomenon:

> *"Religious groups and others view caulbearers differently; however, it is believed that their purpose is to serve mankind, guide people to understand themselves and the world within which we live. Many cultures believe that this makes your child a "King by right" and that he or she has some "special" powers. Those powers can range from leadership abilities to natural healers or having greater insight."*[1]

Now, I don't know if I have special powers, but I have always felt that my purpose was to somehow serve people and be a blessing to them (and I pray I am blessing and serving you through this book). Once I began to come out of the emotional and mental trauma I had experienced, and once I began to manage my grief in a better way, I realized it was time for me to live full out and do *everything* God has called me while I am in this body. If that means write multiple books, then it's time to start writing. If that means traveling the country speaking and preaching, then it's time to get started. I am truly open to what God would have me to do, wherever and whenever He would have me do it.

What about you? Are you living full out? If not, what are you waiting for? This is not a dress rehearsal or a practice, but this life is the actual performance. What gifts, talents and abilities has God given you? Are you using them? If not, it's time, my friend, to use what He gave you. Someone in this world needs the gifts that God has given you, and they are waiting for you to show up in their lives. Just like an audience anxiously awaits the performance of a ballet company, sitting on the edge of their seats in anticipation of what they are about to experience, the world is waiting for you to exercise your gift, in anticipation of what they will receive from God through you. Don't wait a moment longer…step out on faith and do what God has called you to do…NOW. The world is waiting!

Study Question

What gifts, talents and abilities has God given you? What can you do today to begin using them?

―― CONCLUSION ――

Returning to Wholeness: God Can Put Us Back Together Again

Life is a journey; it has its peaks and valleys, its ups and downs. When we enter into the world as infants, we are born into sin and at the same time, we are innocent (in the sense that we've had no experiences that can affect who we believe we are). Then we begin to grow, and life begins to happen. These life experiences can start impacting us emotionally, mentally, and even spiritually, and we begin to lose that innocence we were born with.

The challenges we face in our lives can leave lasting effects upon us. They can be impactful in a negative way, where we become cynical, disappointed, and depressed. Or, they can have a positive effect on us, helping us to grow and mature in ways we never could have imagined. If we believe that everything that happens to us is allowed by God, then we can believe that we will receive something positive from our ordeals. And one of the positives I believe we can receive is wholeness. God can repair our brokenness and can put us back together again. We can become whole again and overcome life's challenges to live a blessed life. This wholeness is found in God and God alone.

Why does God put us back together again? Our brokenness is not without purpose. He does it for His glory! Of course, He wants to bless us and care for us; after all, He is a loving God. But I also believe that God puts us back together again for His glory, because as the God of the Universe, He is to be glorified. Look at the story of Lazarus, who was Jesus' friend (along with his sisters Mary and Martha). Jesus had received word that Lazarus was extremely sick and that his sisters wanted Him to come. Mary and Martha knew that Jesus had the power to heal their brother, so certainly, as their friend, He would come to their aid, and come quickly! However, instead of departing for Mary and Martha's house in Judea right away, He waited two days. When Jesus and the disciples finally arrived, Lazarus had been dead four days. But, before He left for Judea, Jesus said to the disciples, "Lazarus's sickness will not end in death. No, it happened for the glory of God so that the Son of God will receive glory from this." (John 11:4, NLT) Jesus intended for God to get the glory, not from a healing, but from a resurrection!

The rest of the story tells us that Jesus would raise Lazarus from the dead, a greater miracle than anyone could have ever anticipated.

As we look at our broken lives, we see pieces and parts of what was. I was a wife, I was an employee, I was healthy, I was financially stable. But circumstances happened to cause all of these things to seemingly be in the past. The things that made up what we believed was our identity are no longer and we are at a loss as to how to rebuild. I believe that Ezekiel 37 gives us hope and teaches us that God can put us back together again. This may be a familiar story to many Christians, but let's review it.

Ezekiel is a prophet of Israel, who was called by God during the Israelites' exile into Babylon. In chapter 37, God gives Ezekiel a vision of a valley full of dry bones. These were human bones, scattered all over an expansive valley. The bones were very dry (verse 2), which implies that there was no flesh on them and that they had been there for quite some time. God asks Ezekiel whether or not the bones can come back to life. I would imagine Ezekiel, in his mind, wondered to himself, "how in the world can such dry things be given life again?" The situation seems hopeless. But his response to God is "God, you know." For these dry bones to return to life would be a difficult task, and I believe Ezekiel knew that, if it were to happen, it would only be because God enabled them to return to life.

God instructs Ezekiel to prophesy to the bones, and they began to move! Piece by piece, bone by bone, the bones began to be joined to another, then another, then another! (verse 7). Once the bones are together, the flesh, tendons and skin began to appear over the bones, until they looked like human beings. But there was one thing missing; there was still no life in them. God told Ezekiel to prophesy to the wind so that breath would go into these beings. Ezekiel did as God commanded and the lifeless beings became a living and great army! (verse 10) Full and complete life was restored to these bones, who represented the nation of Israel, by the power of God.

What does this story have to do with us who are broken? Our lives have been shattered, and we are left trying to pick up the pieces. Life will probably never be the same for us, and we are wondering what the future will hold. Will I always be alone? Will I always have to struggle with illness? Will I have enough resources to retire? What is going to happen to me? The story of Ezekiel and the dry bones is a message of hope to those of us who are broken: by the power of God, He CAN put us back together again. Ezekiel didn't see how the dry bones could live, but he trusted God and was obedient to His instructions. And as a result, he witnessed dead things come to life. Our own situations may look lifeless, hopeless, fruitless; and it may seem that we are stuck where we are with no way out. But I say this in response to that thought: BUT GOD! God is able to speak a word, and lifeless situations become full of life and hope. God can speak a word and give us hope where there is none. God can speak a word, and just when we thought we could never bear fruit again, a different kind of fruit emerges from our lives. It is the fruit born out of adversity; it is a lasting fruit that can be used to benefit others. And when we use that fruit to help someone else to encourage someone else, to bless someone else, God gets the glory and we become even more fruitful.

God CAN and WILL put us back together again. We must trust God, trust the process that He's taking us through, and be obedient to His instructions. When I lost five family members and a close friend in about a year's time, grief was overwhelming. Coming to the realization that my marriage was over in that same period added to my difficulty. And while I continued to function day by day, I was broken mentally and emotionally.

But, little by little, just when I started to wonder what my future would be, God began to return me to wholeness. Step by step, I saw the pieces of my life come back together again. I am still returning to wholeness in some areas, and there are still some aspects of my life that God continues to work on. But I can see His hand moving in my life. Emotionally and mentally, I am stronger; my faith has increased; and I am living full out again, no longer playing small and hiding the gifts that God has given me. My life is not coming back together again instantaneously, but I can see things are getting better and are falling into place for me. God is doing a work in me as I return to wholeness.

And I can see the fruit that has come as a result of my brokenness, a different kind of fruit: I am able to minister more deeply to people, particularly to those who have experienced death, divorce, and lack. I have a greater sense of compassion for broken people. I have learned to forgive those who have wronged me. And I have learned to trust and believe God in ALL things and for ALL things. For all of this, I must give God glory; without Him, my circumstances would be so different, and I could have become a lonely, bitter, and selfish person.

I pray, as you've read this book, that you now have hope: Hope that God is able to do exceedingly, abundantly, above all we could ever ask or think (Ephesians 3:21). Hope that, although things may look dire now, God is a God of restoration. Hope that your latter will be greater than your former (Haggai 2:9). Hope that God will use your life's circumstances to mature you in the faith and to be a blessing to someone else.

May God continue to bless you as you return to wholeness, so that you can overcome life's challenges and live a blessed life.

---— Epilogue ——

God Loves You

As we recover from the people, things, and situations that have scarred and traumatized us, there is one important fact we must remember - God Loves Us! In our attempts to survive life's challenges, we may lose sight of this. We may wonder what we could have done differently to have avoided such trauma and drama and try not to blame ourselves for what has happened to us; but never lose sight of the fact that God's love for us has not changed and will never change. He loves us in spite of our mistakes, our challenges, our disappointments, and even in spite of ourselves.

God is not a person who loves us because of how well we perform. Of course, God wants us to obey Him and do the things He's called us to do. But we never forfeit God's love because of what we do (or didn't do). God's love is infinite, secure, unchanging…and it is something we can always count on.

As we return to and reclaim our wholeness, reminding ourselves of God's love should be a constant in our lives. We may be struggling to love ourselves at this point because of the mistakes we've made. But the way to start loving ourselves again and believing we are worthy of love is to remember that God loved us first. We do not have the right not to love something or someone that God loves! God is the standard for love, so if I am loved by Him and He considers me loveable, then I can love myself and I, too, can consider myself lovable. If God is able to love me with all of my imperfections, certainly I am able to love myself with all of those same imperfections! God accepts us the way we are!

But bear this in mind; yes, God accepts us the way we are, but He also wants us to become better! Romans 8:29 (NLT) says "For God knew his people in advance, and he chose them to become like his Son, so that his Son would be the firstborn among many brothers and sisters." In other words, God wants us to be transformed into the image and likeness of Jesus. While He accepts us where we are, He desires that we would become more, that we would become better.

Sometimes our brokenness comes from being rejected by people we love but, keep this in mind, God is not like us; He is not a man that He should lie (Numbers 23:19). People are fickle, "sometimey," wishy-washy, unstable (you get the message)! Someone may dislike us because we wore a pretty dress to church one Sunday, because we have something that they desire, or just because! We can't control people's feelings about us and how they react to us, so we can't depend on their love for us to feel secure, confident, and content. Now, we have those ride-or-die friends and family members who are there for us no matter what (if you have these kinds of people in your life, you are blessed). But even our closest and dearest family members and friends can't always be there for us. The one Person who will love us no matter if it's raining or sunny, if we're good or not so good, if we behave correctly or make a mistake is God. And we can depend on that love because it will NEVER change.

Here are some scriptures that can teach us and remind us about the love of God. I encourage you to take some time to meditate on these passages all from the New Living Translation:

Psalm 25:10 - The Lord leads with unfailing love and faithfulness all who keep his covenant and obey his demands.

Psalm 31:7 - I will be glad and rejoice in your unfailing love, for you have seen my troubles, and you care about the anguish of my soul.

Romans 5:5 - And this hope will not lead to disappointment. For we know how dearly God loves us, because he has given us the Holy Spirit to fill our hearts with his love.

Romans 8:38-39 - And I am convinced that nothing can ever separate us from God's love. Neither death nor life, neither angels nor demons, neither our fears for today nor our worries about tomorrow—not even the powers of hell can separate us from God's love. No power in the sky above or in the earth below—indeed, nothing in all creation will ever be able to separate us from the love of God that is revealed in Christ Jesus our Lord.

Galatians 2:20 - My old self has been crucified with Christ. It is no longer I who live, but Christ lives in me. So, I live in this earthly body by trusting in the Son of God, who loved me and gave himself for me.

Ephesians 1:4 - Even before he made the world, God loved us and chose us in Christ to be holy and without fault in his eyes.

Ephesians 3:18-19 - And may you have the power to understand, as all God's people should, how wide, how long, how high, and how deep his love is. May you experience the love of Christ, though it is too great to understand fully. Then you will be made complete with all the fullness of life and power that comes from God.

1 John 4:7-8 - Dear friends, let us continue to love one another, for love comes from God. Anyone who loves is a child of God and knows God. But anyone who does not love does not know God, for God is love.

Most importantly, because God loves us, He sent His one and only Son to the world to die for our sins, so we could be reconciled back to God (John 3:16). Jesus chose to suffer a humiliating and painful death, so that we didn't have to. Understanding the fact that God loves us no matter what can help us recover from our issues and return us to wholeness, so that we can live a blessed life.

Embrace the love God has for you today.

References

Chapter 1
1. Wholeness - A Biblical and Christian Perspective. (n.d.). Retrieved from https://www.faithandhealthconnection.org/the_connection/spirit-soul-and-body/wholeness-biblical-and-christian-perspective/

Chapter 3
1. Perlman, S. (2018, August 27). *What is shalom: the true meaning*. Retrieved from https://jewsforjesus.org/publications/issues/issues-v01-n10/what-is-shalom-the-true-meaning

Chapter 4
1. Baratta, M. (2018, May 27). *Self care 101: 10 ways to take better care of you*. Retrieved from https://www.psychologytoday.com/us/blog/skinny-revisited/201805/self-care-101

Chapter 6
disruptions. 2011. In *Merriam-Webster.com*. Retrieved from https://www.merriam-webster.com/dictionary/disruptions

Chapter 14

1. Degges-White, S. (2018, April 13). *Love bombing: A narcissist's secret weapon.* Retrieved from https://www.psychologytoday.com/us/blog/lifetime-connections/201804/love-bombing-narcissists-secret-weapon

Chapter 15

1. Castro, G. (2013, April 5). *Veiled births: 7 fun facts about this unique phenomenon.* Retrieved from https://mamaslatinas.com/parenting-pregnancy/111944-veiled_births_7_fun_facts

Bibliography

Evans Daniels, M. (2018). *Believe Bigger: Discover the Path to Your Life Purpose.* Audible Edition.

Evans, T. (2014). *Praying Through the Names of God.* Eugene, OR. Harvest House Publishers.

Gonzalez, E. (2019). *The Fierce Urgency of Now.* The Ghost Publishing.

Hawkins, D. (2017). *When Loving Him is Hurting You: Hope and Help for Women Dealing with Narcissism and Emotional Abuse.* Eugene, OR. Harvest House Publishers.

Maxwell, J. (2007). *Failing Forward: Turning Mistakes Into Stepping Stones for Success.* Good Reads Edition.

Rankin, J. (2009). *Spiritual Warfare: The Battle for God's Glory.*

www.ingramcontent.com/pod-product-compliance
Lightning Source LLC
Chambersburg PA
CBHW060359080526
44583CB00012B/391